MW01275038

Tragedy, Truth, Triumph
A Woman's Personal Battle with Loss

Diane Bisson

PublishAmerica
Baltimore

First printing

ISBN: 1-4137-2640-2
PUBLISHED BY PUBLISHAMERICA, LLLP
www.publishamerica.com
Baltimore

Printed in the United States of America

To John, Claude and Michel, who never stopped believing in me.

I want to acknowledge and express my heartfelt gratitude to the contributors of this great miracle.

- My students at St. Charles school and their parents in Sydney, Australia, who believed in me as being a good teacher.
- Ross, Marcelle, Keith, Marilyn, Neville, Barb, Bert, Gladys, and Michelle, my good friends "Down Under" who kept in touch with letters of encouragement, cards, gifts, and telephone calls.
- Bill, my neighbor/writer at the lake, who never tired of giving me advice on writing.
- Dr. Ron, who always made me feel young and attractive when I believed I wasn't.
- Dr. Grant, who showed me what I was all about.
- Dr. Steve, for his honesty.
- My mother, who was always there to share her pearls of wisdom.
- My brother and sister, for their listening ears.
- Lynda, my special friend, who came into my life when I was at my worst.
- Louise, who gave me support and encouragement.
- Pierre, who believed in me, in my talents, and in my future, when I didn't.
- Jeannine (John's mom), who always let me be the me that I could be.
- Pastors Marc and Jeff, who allowed me to feel.
- Chris and Lana, for their patience and their spiritual guidance.
- Pauline, my confidante, my mentor, for her presence, her special love, and her unrelenting spiritual dedication. She never gave up on me.
- John, my best man friend and companion, who touched my heart and who never stopped telling me, "You can do it."
- Claude, my oldest son, who showed me his love by listening, by believing in me, by not being afraid to tell me the truth, and by comforting me.
- Michel, my youngest son, who taught me so many valuable lessons. I felt his presence even when he wasn't there.

- Myself, for accepting God's forgiveness, love, and His Will for my life.
- Jesus.

    Without Him, everything is nothing.
    Without Him, nothing is.
    With Him, nothing is everything!

Contents

Prologue

If you have been victimized by a traumatic experience, be it through a serious affliction, the death of a loved one, a motor vehicle mishap, a broken relationship, rejection, abuse, or even rape, my story may possibly give you strength and hope. However, if you are one of the fortunate ones who has not been forced to live such an experience, you may just learn and begin to understand in a very small way, the insecurities, the agony, and the deepest perplexity of those who have.

It takes a lot of courage and strength to transcend such pain. This courage and strength can only come from one's spiritual side. Pain can be a pathway to our spiritual growth. Physical courage and strength are one thing, but once you redefine your purpose in life, the power within allows you to emerge and to gain mastery over whatever obstacle is placed on your path. The transformation of self can be very frightening at times, but the victories and rewards are innumerable and comforting. Without pain, God would not accomplish all that He desires to do in us and use us as his instruments in the life of others.

Pain is a precursor to change.

Chapter I: In Preparation For...

As I read the first thoughts in my diary and leaf through the pages of our photo album, I get the feeling that maybe this dream was never meant to be, at least not at that time. One sentence in the very first entry turned out to be a lie. As we had said our last good-byes, I had written under the date of December 27,1986, "That was the last of our tears, (we hoped)." The irony of it all is that I've been crying ever since: eight years of tears!

This dream I'm referring to was for me to be accepted in the Teacher Exchange Program for Australia; and for John, my consort, who was to become my husband once we settled in Sydney, it was his wish come true. He had wanted to travel there since his high school days. Having gone through all the red tape and two years in the planning, I was accepted to teach in a private Catholic school in Sydney, Australia. Even at this time, I should have sensed the timing was off. To this day, I still question it.

I was filled with mixed emotions: ecstatic about the opportunity to teach in a different culture, yet troubled by our families' and friends' reactions to this one-year commitment. They all thought we were being extravagant and selfish—extravagant because it was, according to their opinion, going to the other side of the world, and selfish because we were leaving behind our three boys, who were at the time, 24, 20 and 17 years old. They had been invited to come but did not appear to be interested in accompanying us on this educational and exciting adventure. Each had a different reason to decline.

Had these been clear signs, and I simply gave them a blind eye?

Even before we arrived at our destination, we experienced some problems. Our flight from Honolulu to Nadi, Fiji, was delayed two hours because the pilot announced that he had to file a new flight plan so that we could maneuver around a typhoon. We were in Fiji on New Year's Day 1987, but we weren't able to participate in, let alone enjoy the festivities, as we had become the same color as the island's fiery red flowers: we had relaxed by the hotel pool in the afternoon, not realizing we were still getting the sun's rays through an overcast sky. We felt disappointment more than we did the burn.

We landed in Sydney on January 4, 1987. The Australian teacher with whom I had exchanged teaching positions had made temporary living arrangements for us in a motel. John and I had agreed beforehand to look for an apartment ourselves. We were on a budget and knew what we could afford. It wasn't that I had expected the best, but this place was a dump! Two teachers from St. Charles school, Louise and Kerri, who had cordially greeted us at the airport, waving a welcome sign, offered to drive us around the city in order to find a more suitable place. A little worried about not finding one that same evening, we reluctantly decided to leave our luggage at this motel, along with a $100 deposit for the room. It hadn't been too difficult in finding another hotel a little better than this one. Nevertheless, trying to retrieve our luggage along with our deposit had not been so easy. The police had to be called in to sort out the matter. Once we had more or less settled into another hotel, we thought of relaxing over a quiet dinner in the hotel's dining room. It had been a long and frustrating day! It's a good thing that John thought of asking before ordering the meal if they accepted American money because we would have probably ended our evening by washing dishes. The working staff would not accept our currency because they couldn't calculate the exchange. They were even less interested in plastic! We ended our first night in Australia sitting on a bed in a hotel room eating a take-out meal with plastic utensils that the receptionist was kind enough to scrounge for us. Although a minor one, it was still another let-down.

The next day, we started flat hunting. We looked at a few, but there was no way we could have lived like this for an entire year (or so we thought at the time). Some places were run-down and not too clean. The ones we did like were too expensive. That night, as we walked back to the hotel, John must have sensed my disappointment. He stopped under a tree, and he kissed me. I was crying. He told me that things would only get better. If only he had known our fate!

We moved to another hotel the following day, closer to the city, and resumed our search for an apartment. We found a place in Maroubra. It was dingy, and because it had a speck of an ocean view, it was $130.00 a week. That was a lot of money for us at the time (considering this was 17 years ago), and we were reaching a point of desperation. We would have taken this one, had we been allowed to paint it. The landlord refused it. We decided against it.

Another blow!

We were realizing that renting in Sydney was not cheap, and besides that, we didn't have any furniture or cookware. All we had brought with us were our clothes. A few apartments we had looked at were more or less furnished— less was more like it. We then looked into the cost of renting furniture and basic items of some cookware. We took a taxi to PABS Renting Place on the other side of the city, only to learn that we would have to pay $1800 for 4 pieces of furniture. This was just for renting them for a year. It had not been a good idea after all.

Back in the hotel room that evening, I received a telephone call from Marie, one of the mothers from St. Charles school where I had been assigned to teach. She was kind enough to offer us two single mattresses once we found a place to live. Apartment hunting went on for a few days, and even though we had met some very nice people, always ready to help us, we were getting very tired and dispirited. We had been in Sydney for six days now, we still had not settled in, and the school's first semester was just around the corner. Hotel prices were getting too steep for our budget. It was on January 10, 1987, that I became very worried and started second-guessing this adventure. What had I done? What was I doing here? I was very homesick that evening. I cried myself to sleep.

Finally on January 12, (thanks to Marie and her husband Chris) we found what was to be our home for a year. It was a furnished apartment on Ocean Street in Bondi. Our rental problems were over! Our carefully-planned dream was to begin, or so we thought. After being approved by the rental agency and paying the required security bond on the flat, we moved in and started cleaning the place. We wanted to give it a fresh scent, and we rearranged the furniture to suit our liking. What a big mistake that turned out to be! It just so happened that on that same evening we had been invited for dinner at Keith's and Marilyn's house (a great couple with two nice kids, Sharne and Keiran, who all became our good friends). On our return from their place, at the flick of the hallway lights, we found ourselves in "Cockroach City!" We were later informed that by cleaning our apartment, we had disturbed these ugly, repulsive creatures. They were all over: in the carpet, climbing up the walls, crawling on the kitchen counter, even flying in, as the windows didn't have any screens. I covered my head, in fear of having some of them land in my hair. John must have killed hundreds of them with some leftover cleaning spray, and with the two swords he had been conned into buying as souvenirs from Suva, Fiji. By pure coincidence, we discovered they rested when the lights were off. Needless to say, I did not close my eyes that night. I thought out loud, "This must be one of the drawbacks of living 'Down Under.'"After lodging the complaint with the rental agent by showing him a dustpan full of the tiny beasts, the apartment was fumigated the next day.

Back home in Canada in 1984, John and I had traveled through the majestic, breathtaking Rocky Mountains on our Harley motorcycle. What a thrilling way to see, to feel, to smell, and to experience nature! As both of us felt that it was an excellent and more economical way to do our touring of Australia, we decided to ship our bike to Sydney. It took a lot of doing, but we got it there. Once it arrived, John had to put up with a few hassles: running around to different freight shipping yards before locating the right one to claim the bike, going through the red tape of its identification and registration, also purchasing motorcycle insurance, as well as New South Wales license plates. Finally, the bike was released, ready to be picked up in Yagoona. Ross and Marcelle, who today are some of our best friends "Down Under," offered to drive us there to unpack the crate, and John would ride it back to Bondi. He was a little concerned about riding it on the opposite side of the road, as that is the way it's done over there.

On January 21, we picked up the Harley. It was raining of course…that's the way our course of events was unfolding. That day was the beginning of the end of our dream, and the birth of an incessant nightmare!

Chapter II: The Encounter

The dream of teaching in Australia and experiencing a different culture, enjoying new friends, and discovering a new country, hardly had a chance to unfold. My first day at St. Charles school was February 2. I met the school personnel who seemed friendly enough. The following day was much better because I was introduced to my 28 fourth-graders, a super group of kids. I loved them from the minute I met them. After my 24 years in the teaching profession, and being comfortable with the Canadian educational system, I found it a bit unnerving getting accustomed to theirs. Nevertheless, I was looking forward to exchanging teaching strategies. Somehow my dedication and efforts became fruitless. I felt insecure many times; I was rapidly losing my self-confidence, something I had never experienced throughout my career before this time. I prayed and asked the good Lord to give me the strength and the encouragement I needed to go on. My prayer was answered. I was able to persevere. As I'm reading my diary, most of my entries following that plea with God begin with the phrase, "Another good day!"

Unfortunately, that positive feeling did not last too long. The school climate was becoming a bit too regimented. Being more of a liberal and free-spirited teacher, and one who believes in guiding the student to experiment and to make discoveries on his own, I thought I would introduce some of my own teaching strategies that had proven to be successful back home in Ontario. Paul, the school principal, was very uncomfortable with my teaching philosophy, and he disagreed. I had to do it their way. I tried hard to conform to this new method; after all, I was a visitor in the school and had to respect their ways. It was contrary to my training and to my teaching beliefs. I felt I was teaching these students with methods that, to me, were archaic. The dissatisfaction with my work soon became apparent in my relationship with John, with my colleagues, friends and acquaintances. I became disinterested. My days in class felt long and demanding (something I had never before experienced in 24 years of teaching). When I had the chance to relax, I preferred to be alone and quiet. The irony of it all was that we were supposed to be living an adventure…a perfect time to meet new and different people and to visit as many places as time would allow us. Were we not there to try to saturate ourselves with the country's culture and its customs? This was not happening. I was slowly creeping into a self-made protective shell.

Tuesday, March 3, 1987, was a day of revelation for me. I had been asked to be at school that evening to present and to explain to the parents of my students my objectives for the coming school year. I had never been nervous talking to or discussing with parents, but because of the still existing controversy over some of my tactics used in my teaching, I felt very concerned about how these parents would accept me, first of all as an individual, then as a teacher. As I look back on this, I can picture it so vividly. After my presentation, which lasted over an hour, the parents asked many questions. My first reaction to all their questions was that maybe they weren't totally convinced of these so-called "new Canadian" and "Diane-made" teaching methods. Or was it that they just didn't feel comfortable with my philosophy as an educator? Well, I was wrong.

Once I had answered all of their questions, one mother stood up and started applauding me. Another mother stood up and did the same. She was followed by a couple who joined in until all the parents were standing up and applauding in unison. Only to add to their obvious acceptance of my curriculum goals as their child's teacher were these comforting and complimentary remarks expressed by one couple and another father. They came up to me while everyone had reconvened in the hallway for wine and cheese (here in Ontario, it's coffee and doughnuts), and the mother said, "Miss, you're a breath of fresh air in our school. Thank you." Another father followed and added, "Keep doing whatever you're doing. The kids love you."

For the first time since school had started, this testimony had confirmed the belief I had in myself as being a competent teacher and doing good work with the children. Now I felt reassured. However, that feeling didn't last too long: six short days. The following Monday, March 9, Paul, the school's principal, called me into his office, wherein he implied that I appeared to be on some sort of mission. He accused me of being a threat to some of the experienced teachers on staff and intimidating the younger ones by "showing off" my new ways of teaching children. He didn't ask, but told me to discontinue my methods and ordered me to return to theirs.

That night, I made up my mind to try my best, but with a promise to myself of being on the first flight back home at the end of this first semester if the situation did not improve. Somehow things did not turn out that way. I contacted Toni, the exchange representative, and explained my dilemma. She referred me to Jennifer and Peter, two members of the Catholic Education Office. They were to investigate my situation at St. Charles. We met at school on March 23, and after some short discussion, Peter offered me a position in the Special Education Services Department, which was in my field of expertise. While parting, they both expressed their concern with, "We understand how you must feel. We're very sorry this happened." How little did they know how I felt! I was devastated! I felt like a failure! Why couldn't the school personnel acknowledge some of my ways? Were my methods…was I so different? I wanted to say to them, "Please don't tell me you know how I feel. You're not in my situation. You couldn't know!" I refrained from doing so. I was in enough of a mess.

A few days later, I was invited to visit Jennifer's country school. (She was the principal.) This was my dream school. I had always envisioned starting my own little school out in the country somewhere, surrounded by mountains and water, and having animals and a garden. Opening such a school for underprivileged children was my plan following retirement. Jennifer introduced me to the students, and I could feel her evaluating my rapport with them. I felt so much at ease. I was in my element.

I worked with Kristina, who had a lateral lisp, and with Jessica, a Down's Syndrome child. At that moment, I made my decision to leave St. Charles and to accept a position with the Special Education Department. This was the area where I was at my best. This is what I wanted to do. This was me! My interview for a new school was scheduled for Thursday, April 2 at 9:00 a.m. I never made it.

Ironically, not having been informed of my decision to leave St. Charles to accept a different teaching position, the school's committee of parents and friends had organized an evening in the school's gymnasium to welcome all the new families in the school, and to introduce me, the Canadian teacher who was replacing one of their own. It was to be a casual, easy-going, and laid-back affair, just like most of their gatherings. Yes, what you read and hear about Australians is true; they are friendly, laid-back and easy-going individuals, except in one area of their life, which I will explain later. The festivities included a picnic-like format, whereby the parents, students, nuns, and teaching staff brought their own picnic basket and blankets and sat on the gymnasium floor. Since the dress code was casual, John and I jumped into our jeans and picked up a pizza at Elmo's Place (another good friend) and decided to go to the event on the Harley. The gymnasium exuded a warm atmosphere. Everyone was friendly and relaxed. The evening ended with a bush dance to the tone of country music and square dancing. The parents danced with each other, with friends, and with their own children. John even had a few dances with some of my students and with Sister Clare. Everyone had "good fun" (an expression often used over there). It had been a gratifying evening. At 10:30 p.m., we gathered our belongings, as it was time to leave. We had church services in the morning, and the children were getting tired. John and I were outside putting on our bike gear, when a few of the parents and their children walked over to admire our motorcycle. Some fathers asked John how it felt riding in Oz as compared to riding in Canada, while some of the mothers were puzzled as to why I wasn't afraid or traveling in such a fashion. Since we were avid bike enthusiasts, and it was still early, we decided, as we were leaving the school grounds, to take a short ride into the city to admire and appreciate all the different night lights. Sydney is much more beautiful in the evening. Little did we know that the lights would be turned off!

The diary that our boys had given us as their going-away present bears on its leather cover a gold-colored plaque with the engraving, "Australian Encounter '87." I guess I had taken for granted then that the word "encounter" simply meant "a greeting with." As I decided to write my story, I was curious of the word's meaning, and I verified it. Webster's dictionary defines the word "encounter" as:

- to meet as an adversary or enemy
- to engage in conflict with,
- to come upon face to face,
- to come unexpectedly,
- a sudden or violent clash.

I can't seem to find the precise words to explain how shocked I was after reading all those befitting definitions. These explanations are all applicable to what ensued. This is where my story actually begins.

The "Australian Encounter" has changed my priorities, my values, my aspirations, my feelings, my soul, my behavior, my performance as a mother, daughter, sister, partner, teacher and friend; it also has had a significant impact on my way of thinking, my perceptions, my awareness to life's critical issues, my outlook on life—changes that came about for the betterment of my whole being. My shattered dream has been rerouted into a future that leads me

18

toward the loving arms of God. However, this reconditioning, this overhaul, this tune-up, this realignment took eight long, painful, testing, struggling, refining years. I did not realize it then that emotional, physical, and psychological pain, but most importantly spiritual strength, were to become the most powerful forces in molding the course of the rest of my life.

This encounter I'm referring to manifested itself on the evening of March 28, 1987, when John and I left the school yard. Not even fifteen minutes later, we became the victims of a horrific motor vehicle accident. I'm sorry to say that this is the only time Australians are not laid-back or easy-going. Once they get behind the wheel of a car, they become totally aggressive! It isn't necessary to get into the ugly details of its happenings (to this day I don't remember the collision), only that liability had never been an issue; we were hit by an unlicensed, drunk driver, who ran a red light, and we both suffered numerous serious injuries. I won't focus on the physical impairments I sustained, but without a doubt, they did set limitations on my life, and, to this day, still do.

Not only am I putting these thoughts down on paper for my own therapeutic need in trying to find the appropriate words to sort through the issues of guilt and punishment, to explain and understand my feelings, but I'm also hoping that my story, possibly a small part of it, or even just one sentence, can serve as a catharsis not only for me, but also for you, dear reader. If my story helps you, I am pleased. However, if it does not, I will remain pleased because while writing it, I developed, and was, with God's grace, able to cultivate an inner awareness of tranquillity and to rebuild my life with a purpose. "I can comfort those in any trouble with the comfort 'I myself' have received from God" (2 Corinthians 1:3,4).

Chapter III: Masking

My stay in the hospital was a difficult one. Bed-ridden for three weeks, I felt helpless. I could not enjoy all of the attention I was getting, especially from well-wishing parents, students, colleagues and the few friends we had met. I felt total embarrassment! However, I did make an effort of showing them my appreciation, even though most of the time I felt like crying, even screaming. I wanted to be left alone. At times, when I was being pessimistic, these well-meaning visitors would show their compassion by saying, "We understand; we know how you feel." And I would want to reply, "Please, don't tell me you know how I feel. You're not in my body; you're not inside my head; you're not in my situation; therefore, you couldn't know!"

To this day, I feel that this hardship has kept John in captivity and in bondage. From the very first day after my discharge (almost a month later, after learning how to hop on one leg with the support of two crutches and a neck brace), I felt like I had become his excess baggage to lug around. He too was in a lot of pain, but because of his pride, I suppose, and the fact that he must have felt he had to be the strong one, he would hide it under his solid carapace and his mask. I simply couldn't do that. I first sensed his anger toward this disappointment, which had turned into a nightmare on the evening of April 29, when both of us tried to hug each other, not only out of love, but also out of disappointment and sorrow, only to discover that we were both in too much pain to do so. I sensed his rage at what then appeared to be meaningless suffering.

Preceding uncontrollable circumstances had forced me to become independent, to learn to do my own thing, as a while back, I had entered the state of widowhood at the young age of 39 and was left with the responsibility of raising and providing for a 14- and a 18-year-old; and at this point, six years later, my dependence on John for almost everything, from preparing my meals to having him sit me on a hospital chair inside the shower stall to wash my hair, was all foisted upon me. I had become a culprit of helplessness. It was total humiliation!

I started feeling like a nuisance, a burden to others; and to myself, I was worthless, a big NOTHING! My injuries had consumed my confidence, my self-respect, and my pride. I was gradually crawling back into my cocoon. I felt a great need to isolate myself from people. I did not want to see or to talk to anyone, let alone answer my telephone calls. John was growing tired of making excuses for me, even lying at times. I was living in conflict between loneliness and my desire to be left alone to taste isolation. My solitude became as crucial to me as the air I was breathing. I did not want to go anywhere. How many times John was forced to politely decline numerous invitations from so many good people! He could have gone, and would have, but he worried about leaving me alone. When I think of those times now, I realize that's when the guilt started growing inside of him—the guilt of shipping the Harley to Sydney. Only a few days ago (being a little over eight years now) did he tell me that every time he saw me limping or crying in pain, he felt partly responsible. His explanation was, "You wouldn't be like this today if it wasn't for me." Little did he realize, let alone believe, that had I not had that encounter, my life would probably have remained the same. Only because of living in my own Hades am I now able to taste a piece of Heaven.

The arguments were becoming greater in number and closer together. John's way of coping, if one can call it coping, was to give me the silent treatment. Not only did I find it hard to heal with the physical pain, but at this point, my insides were rapidly being ripped apart by his evasion. I just wanted to go home to be with my loved ones, and home was where I should have stayed, I thought. I had made so many mistakes in my life, but the good Lord had forgiven me. Was He still willing to do it? Mea culpa! Mea culpa! I was drawing closer to Him with a contrite heart (Psalm 51:7-9).

I was still whipping myself, feeling like a failure again, and given the chance, I would have started all over again, doing things differently. I guess most people feel that way at some crossroads in their life. Whenever these feelings of blame and remorse encroached my privacy, I would often reflect on this passage from one of my readings:

> I wish there were some wonderful place
> called the Land of Beginning again
> where all our mistakes and all our heartaches
> and all our poor selfish grief

could be dropped like a shabby old coat at the door
and never to be put on again.

—Robert Frost

Today, I can say that I have found that place: in the arms of God.

The idea of returning to Canada was out of the question. The doctors had told me that the 23-hour flight would be more than I could tolerate. It was early May when the orthopaedic surgeon informed me that I could possibly return at the end of October. The end of October! That was five months away! My whole world crumbled again! Was this really happening? Could it be just a bad dream from all the pain medication I was taking? Or maybe I was in a coma? Was I hallucinating? Why couldn't I be home with my family?

These many questions had become a series of invocations and supplications. I was mentally writing my own Book of Lamentations! It brought back some painful memories of my convent days when the congregation would join together in the chapel for the mournful recital of litanies. I was now reliving this same ceremonial, only this time the prayer consisted of my own formulated incantations: "God, where are you? Have you forgotten me? Look, I'm here. I'm hurting! I'm in pain! Please, help me!"

The doctors sympathized, "We understand. We know how you feel." And again I wanted to scream, "You don't know how I feel! How could you? You don't have my pain. You don't feel the hurt and the disappointment." From that point on, everything became a monotonous routine. John would take me for my daily walk, (if you can call hopping on one leg, holding two crutches and wearing a neck brace enjoying a walk). If I didn't have to force myself to socialize with people, even with our good friends, I would have to submit and accept John's diligent care of my needs: bringing me for my physiotherapy treatments, cooking meals, doing laundry, grocery shopping, and running errands. Most evenings were spent sitting in bed, watching television, more than not, staring at the tube. I had tried reading, but it only exacerbated my headaches. The now mundane and dull activities had been going on for two long months. Our well-planned exciting adventure had now transpired into an everyday performance of an established protocol. Our life had taken the quality of a bad dream.

One afternoon in June, as I was getting ready for my daily stroll, I tried putting on my navy pair of slacks and was forced to accept the reality that they would never make it up my thighs. I thought my regimen had been enough exercise to help me keep fit. On my next visit for physiotherapy, I asked Gillian to weigh me. 128 lbs! I had gained 16 pounds since the accident. It just couldn't be! But it was! My revenge on food had made its appearance. I soon discovered that only a few pieces of clothing fitted me. Added to my feelings of nothingness, boredom, frustration, depression and dependency was now one of ugliness! Applying make-up on my face became a chore in vain. I was trying to produce something fake. Looking in the mirror, I saw myself ageing: rings under my eyes, eyes that revealed emptiness and listlessness. No eyeshadow could hide that! Apart from having my graying face, blemished by dry, blotchy lesions, it also lacked expression, and when I did manage to smile, I looked so phony, so artificial, so plastic. I reminded myself of a mannequin on display. I used to appreciate the cliché, "Women are like fine wine; as they age, they get better." But then I had to ask myself, "They get better than what?" I just wanted to die! That's when I started drinking a little more than my usual glass of wine with dinner. I climbed into the bottle of whiskey and tried drowning myself in it, hoping to reach oblivion; instead, I became more and more disheartened by the minute. John was doing his best to render our situation more endurable, but I was right out of it. The so-called "heavy disputes" had now turned into seething arguments. I would cry, scream, and had even started throwing things. I would have needed a "scream chamber." I became so angry and bitter. I couldn't channel or dissipate it in a harmless way. It seemed I had nothing to look forward to. I didn't have my health, and I couldn't do what I loved most—teach; I missed it so much. My relationship with John had grown into a volatile and steaming, emotional volcano, and I was 14,000 miles away from home and family!

John didn't know how to handle me. He could no longer bear to listen to my loss of hope, so he entered me into a counseling program. The sessions were helpful, until the day the therapist became a little annoyed with my crying episodes and hostile attitude. He made the mistake of telling me that he understood how I felt and that it was high time I started reconstructing my negative thoughts into positive ones. How could I do that when I felt I had nothing worthwhile going for me? And besides, he didn't have a clue on how or what I was feeling. I ranted at him, "How dare you say you know how I feel! How could you? You're not in my body, feeling my pain! You're not inside my head with my thoughts! You're not in my heart, feeling my emotions! So, don't tell me you know and understand how and what I feel!" That was my last session.

The light became even dimmer on June 25, when following my regular visit with the orthopaedic surgeon, I was told I could not teach for the remainder of the school year. If someone had carved out a hole in my stomach, I probably would have been able to deal with the pain, because that kind heals with time. But to be told that I could not work with my students of only seven weeks left me with an unexplainable feeling. What was this new emotion called? I couldn't give it a name. I don't know if there exists a specific word to describe what I felt then: it was emptiness, failure, defeat, shame, sadness, guilt, anguish, alienation, loneliness, fear, futility, self-hatred all bottled into one. This announcement translated into the introit to my personal requiem.

That evening, John shared my feeling of thwarted expectation. He knew how much I loved teaching. He held me gently in his arms and empathized with me, "I know how you must feel." And again, I said to myself, "Please, don't tell me you know how I feel. You couldn't know! You're not the one going through this; I am."

Chapter IV: On Surrendering

It was June 29 that I first made true contact with God after backsliding for so many years. Unless God is revealed to us through personal experience, we can never really know God. Many of us know about God; we know who He is; we know His story, but that's quite different from knowing God. It is one thing to be introduced to a person, but quite another to know that individual personally.

Throughout this turmoil, I had become so distressed and so negative that I had forgotten about my Father in Heaven. Satan had taken a firm hold of me for all that time. I had allowed him to incapacitate me. But on this day, after I had announced to my students that I could not resume my teaching duties, I hopped over to the church across the street from the school yard, lit a candle, asked God's forgiveness for my apostasy, and I placed all my beautiful nine-year-old students under His protection. The flicker of light that radiated from the burning candle somehow reached my soul at that very moment and illuminated me in a very special way. I felt God's presence there close to me. I realized that I had not communicated with Him in such a long time.

Time went slowly. I was growing more and more impatient with the physical healing. In the following months, I managed to walk with both legs and one crutch for support; then I graduated to a walking cane. On July 28, we met our solicitor, who informed us that it would probably take over two years to settle our accident claim. It sounded promising, considering the seriousness of it all and all its complexities, but we still needed to share the disappointment of our shattered dreams. Trying to reassure us, he said, "It's so unfortunate this happened. I know how devastated you must be feeling." Once more, I felt and urge of crying out, "Please don't tell us you know how we feel! You don't have the foggiest idea of how we feel." We left his office somewhat relieved that our case would not drag on for too long. Little did we know what the future held in store for us.

My last visit to the doctor was an encouraging one. Due to the fact that we had been more or less confined to our apartment for five months, with not too much distraction and that we couldn't go home for another month, he recommended that we leave Sydney and take an easy and relaxing holiday before returning to Canada. He felt a short trip might compensate for our fulfilment of not having been able to tour the country on our Harley as much as we had anticipated. The holiday had to be planned carefully because of our injuries. We could not even entertain the thought of taking a short flight somewhere, due to our now reduced funds. We opted to rent a Budget camper-style van, which would eliminate motel costs and allow us to stop and rest whenever there was a need. We did get to visit and enjoy a few interesting places, some of which became therapeutic. I recall sitting in Mataranka's natural hot springs, appreciating the steady rhythm of the soothing warm current of water lapping against my back and my hip. During the course of our journey, we did stop twice for physiotherapy treatments on my back and neck. It was now just the two of us trying to enjoy ourselves on our own time the best way we could. We paced ourselves in regards to what we could do without feeling any obligation to explain to, or humor people. We were able to drop the masks and the roles we had feigned to please our well-meaning friends. Many times we cried together. Nevertheless, this holiday, or as I prefer to call it, this get-away-from-it-all time, provided us with serenity, solace, and release. For the first time since that dreadful evening in March, we were able to laugh wholeheartedly.

On our arrival back to Sydney, it was a sad and poignant time to bid farewell to my students and their parents, to all of our good friends we had made. With many of them, we had become kindred spirits. We thanked them for all they had done for us, and as we boarded the plane, we were both silent, for we realized that we might never see these caring and giving people again. As it was not a busy flight, the airline was kind enough to allow me to use two seats in the rear of the plane, as I needed to stretch and lie down quite often. In doing so, and taking the pain-easing medication, I was able to manage the 23 hours of flight time without too much discomfort. The presentiment of seeing my family, or at least some of them at the airport, helped me to disregard my pain. Finally, I had something to look forward to!

We landed at Toronto International Airport on the last week of October, just as the doctors had advised. I remember hurrying along with my crutches while still wearing my neck brace. (The doctors had suggested that I use both crutches for the trip, especially for walking around a busy airport.) I couldn't wait to see a familiar face! Would it be my sons, or one of them, or maybe my brother, my mother or again my sister and her husband? Such was not the case as far as any family member of mine was concerned. After claiming our baggage, we were welcomed by John's son and one of John's buddies. Where were my people? I couldn't believe it! No one was there! Had I not been gone for close to a year and badly traumatized in a serious motor vehicle accident? Couldn't someone have made an effort of being there to welcome me and to give me a comforting hug?

As I reflect back on this, I still tremble inside; I can still feel the emptiness I experienced at that time. Just then, I started feeling sorry for myself. The "poor me" and the "nobody cares" thoughts were choking me. I wanted to cry, but somehow couldn't. I wanted to scream, but felt that no sound would come out. While John was laughing and sharing with Michael and Ed, I felt desolate and forgotten. I later learned that my family members had different reasons for not being at the airport: no ride to get there, working the night shift, had to stay home with the kids, concerned about how I would look and being uncomfortable facing me. (Some members, especially my mother, had pictured me arriving home in a wheelchair as a cripple with only one leg, even though, to reassure them that I was all right, I had sent some photos of myself standing on my two legs resting on my walking cane.) It took a long time, but I was able to forgive them.

On the first weekend home, John's parents invited both families to participate in the official "Welcome home, John and Diane," party. Some of the aunts and uncles, nephews and nieces hugged us for a long time, while others cried as they greeted us. We handed out all of the carefully selected souvenirs we had brought back for them. We thanked everyone for their "get well" cards and letters sent to St. Vincent's hospital in Sydney, and for coming over that evening. I made a point of telling them how John deserved a medal or some kind of trophy for having taken such good care of me during my convalescence. I became very emotional, and I broke down in tears. Everyone became quiet and uncomfortable. The excitement, the joy and laughter that had dominated over the room were suddenly transformed into a sombre mood. Then, one of John's aunts said, "It's okay to cry, Diane. We understand. We can sympathize, and we know how you feel." Again, I stopped myself from saying, "Please, don't tell me you know how I feel! You don't feel the disappointment that is in my heart!"

Chapter V: Existing:
Going Through the Motions

How quickly people went on with their daily activities! From that point on, I guess everyone assumed that we would put the accident behind us (which I guess we should have done), heal, return to our regular jobs, and life would return to normal. How I wished it would have been that easy, that uncomplicated! It wasn't. I felt tremendous pressure from myself and from others to surmount my injuries. It was expected of me to take on a spouse's and mother's responsibilities. I was to simply jump back into the same roles, excluding, of course, the one of a teacher. I don't know if people felt disdain toward my appearance or if it was simply an uncomfortable and awkward feeling to be in my presence, but their avoidance left me with a feeling of neglect. I guess my friends and some family members were at a loss for words to encourage and comfort me. The apprehension I felt from both families only added to my sentiment of isolation. I still remember the few times when John's daughter and my two nephews were hesitant in approaching me every time they felt they had to give me a hug. I guess they stayed away because they didn't want to hurt me physically, but I still felt ignored and cheated of their once tender and sincere caresses. We were seldom invited for dinner and were rarely visited or telephoned to check on how we were doing. I knew we weren't the outgoing couple we once were, and I surely wasn't my bubbly "old self," but we still had many interesting things to talk about and to share, apart from the accident: we had lived in Australia for the last 10 months!

I look back on New Year's Day 1988. A brand new year! Surely our situation would ameliorate. Unfortunately, John was experiencing much difficulty in handling his regular work week, and I was still home praying for the day I would return to teaching. I was in physiotherapy twice a week, looking forward to the day when I wouldn't feel the unrelenting pain, and when I could be my "old self" again. However, my pain threshold was still low, and my patience even lower. By now, my 24-year-old son had moved out of the province to the big city culture and opportunities, and I was more or less forced to tell my 20-year-old to start looking for his own place, as I found myself "playing" mom again by doing laundry for three, cooking for three, and preparing lunches for him and for John. Being the kind of person who has much difficulty saying no, I found myself overdoing it with the household chores and paying the price "pain wise" for days following. Prior to leaving for this adventure, the three boys had agreed to live together in my mother's small house, which we had rented for them. My oldest son had been placed in charge of things. After a while, John's 17-year-old had decided to move out because he and my youngest son could not get along. As he did not want to return to live in the country with his mother, he moved in with one of his aunts, John's older sister, who was charitable enough to take him in. On our return, he had expected to move in with us (which was the plan had the accident not happened), but now that I had asked my own son to move out because I couldn't handle the extra work load, I could not accept Michael. The feeling of culpability was so strong inside of me; it was like a beast ripping my entrails, gobbling them up piece by piece. I knew it was my only solution if I wanted to heal, but I still felt selfish. Today I know I wasn't being egoistic, but rather taking care of myself in order to function normally again. However, some members of the family did not view it that way; they went out of their way to relay to people that, "Diane uses her pain and her injuries to suit her situation. She only wants to be left alone." They went as far as naming me, "the selfish b—." The malicious gossip spread like wild fire, so much so that I became too embarrassed to attend family gatherings. I felt ostracized and alienated from everyone. I could not pretend to be happy, and I surely didn't have the incentive to be gracious. I was again turning into a recluse. The Diane who once savoured adventure, challenges, hosting fancy dinner parties, mingling and dancing had become a timid, introverted, almost agoraphobic individual. When I did find myself comfortable with other acquaintances, the issue would sometimes make its way into the conversation. By then, I had recovered from the crying episodes. I had now entered the angry stage. I had become a bitter person. My voice would quiver, and I would feel my body tremble as I tried to explain and to justify my position as I felt I had an obligation and every right to do so. In trying to calm me down, these caring and concerned people would often say to me, "Diane, you have every right to feel that way. We understand. We know how you feel." Most times, I could control myself and accept the comment. Other times, I would repudiate it and turn their words of intended comfort into suspicious accusations. I would become very jittery and simply lash out, "Please, don't tell me you know how I feel! How could you know? Are you living in this nightmare? You're not in my body! You couldn't know!" This repetition of my request was starting to sound like a script of memorized lines from a play. Oswald Chambers wrote, "Suffering either makes fiends of us or it makes saints of us; it depends entirely on our relationship towards God." I had become that fiend! I was angry at the world. I was angry at God!

That year when John and I lived alone in the small cottage we had bought along Lake Erie, I took the role of a zombie, definition being, "a person held to resemble the so-called walking dead." I simply existed. I had become the fragile shell of someone else. I was haphazardly wandering through life. I was going through the motions.

A full day for me was making myself look presentable, bringing in the mail, having a glimpse at the local newspaper, lying down in the afternoon making an effort to prepare dinner, only to end the day by retiring early from total exhaustion. Everything took so much effort. It wasn't what you would call an enriching day! I would stare out of our large living room window facing the lake, wondering what was happening to me and what lay ahead. I was engrossed in a feeling of ennui. I couldn't get involved in any kind of interest. My concentration was limited. My memory was poor. My headaches were excruciating. I would more or less plug myself in, sitting on a heating pad for hours. I couldn't get interested in television. I had done enough of that in Sydney. The medication wasn't helping much. I became so desperate in trying to palliate the boredom of a sedate life that one day I found myself arranging toothpicks. Can you believe it? I was placing all of the pointed ends at the bottom of the holder. Was that deranged or what? My sedentary life was turning me into an irrational being. I felt so guilty for not doing anything productive. Was I succumbing to my condition? Why could I not get a grip on myself? It had been long enough now.

I had wasted enough time in this deep and dark abyss. It wasn't a grave, even though I wished it had been. I felt entombed in feelings of darkness. I had become hermit-like. I didn't know how to get myself back to the Land of the Living. I needed some kind of electrode to jump-start my body! I was stuck in a life that was askew and lopsided. I started having anxiety attacks. I would hyperventilate, then lose consciousness. This went on for one year and a half. That summer, I was hospitalized for one week, and I underwent different tests identifying my fainting episodes as pseudo-seizures. Following that, my family doctor who had been assigned to my case since my return to Canada referred me to a psychiatrist. The timing was perfect, as I had started giving up on myself and on my life. It took countless visits before I was able to emerge from my pit of despair. I had become such a negative person, mostly because I did not feel useful or productive. I couldn't escape the clutches of guilt. I was needed by my loved ones, but I wasn't able to give. I needed to feel like a mother again; I needed to dedicate myself to my work, and to my students. I longed to be in the educational field again. I asked the good Lord to inspire me, and He did. Since my memory and my concentration had been more or less in a state of limbo for quite some time, I decided to pursue post-university studies. I had nothing to lose. It would keep me occupied and the work load would activate my brain cells. Since the medical profession had speculated the strong probability of my not being capable of teaching full-time again, I enrolled into Waterloo's University correspondence program in social work, sociology, and psychology. My choice of these courses was based on the possibility of becoming a youth counselor or a social worker. Having suffered a head injury in the accident, I experienced much difficulty with the assignments. My final marks did not mirror my usual grades, but I still managed to obtain credits during three school terms.

We were now entering the summer of '89, and the insurance company and I were discussing various ways of handling my employment situation. (I had been on a long term disability pension.) We were designing a plan for my reintegration into the work force—teaching that is, on a part-time basis. It felt so good just talking about the possibility of working again! Everyone involved in the process was in agreement: the insurance company, my doctors, the school board, the school's principal, and John. I myself was in disbelief! The medical authorities had assumed I would never teach again, and there I was returning to my duties in September. Was this God's plan for me? In September of '89, I began teaching three alternate days per week. Having been away from routines, commuting back and forth, deadlines, commitments, meetings, interviews with parents, working with children and colleagues, preparing lessons, using stairs, standing and/or sitting for too long a time, I was unable to handle the pressure and the stress. I was forced to leave at the end of October of that same year. I felt like a failure. That word again! Would it ever be obliterated from my vocabulary? Failure enrobed my whole being! I had disappointed and cheated everyone.

I wallowed in self-pity until December, when a principal from a one-level school contacted me and offered me a position, which I would share with another teacher in the role of Learning Resource teacher. He said to me, "Diane, your reputation as being one of our better teachers precedes you. I have faith in you. I'm almost certain you can fill in this role description and do a good job. Are you willing to try it?" It sounded too good to be true. After some serious consideration and a lengthy discussion with my physician, I accepted. Was 1990 to be my year of comeback? As far as teaching was concerned, yes, it was. It turned out to be *my* year. The pain in my body was rapidly being camouflaged by my deep involvement in my work. My dedication had grown into an obsession which had surpassed its parameters. Teaching had turned into a placebo (Latin for "I shall please"), and I had grown addicted to it. My goal was to prove myself to the school authorities, to my students and their parents, to my colleagues, to my doctors, to the insurance company, to my family, my friends, and to John…I guess to everyone I knew, that I could still be the teacher I once was, if not a better one. My self-esteem was back. I became a workaholic. Being of Type A personality, I had to contend with my obsessive and oppressive perfectionism, which made onerous and rigorous demands on my body. I had become a teaching addict! Little did I know at the time that my addiction was already creating demands and pressures that would later harvest into a self-transformation. Teaching was my credo! I had lost sight of who I was. My identity was totally wrapped up in my work. I felt most alive when I was teaching. My self-worth was overwhelmingly swathed in my performance as a teacher. I had turned the school milieu into my home away from home, so to speak. The time-worn axiom, "Home is where the heart is," suited me just fine. My life clicked like a metronome. I had orchestrated my time and choreographed my steps in order to achieve their maximum effect. I was there every morning at 8 a.m. and seldom left the building before 5:30 p.m. Once home, I would rush into preparing and eating dinner, and if I didn't have a meeting with parents, a workshop or the like, I always managed to find an excuse to work in my books. There really wasn't much time to spend with John or my family, let alone time to relax, or so I believed at the time. Nevertheless, I would look forward to the weekends for relaxation and quiet time. But for John, it was a different story. John, being of a gregarious nature, would suggest doing things, going here and there, visiting family and friends, or inviting so and so, and I just didn't want it. I enjoyed our quiet time at home.

My body spoke to me in the only language it knew—the language of pain emitting cues to take precautions. It was barraged with S.O.S messages, and I was ignoring them. I became deaf to its taunting and rebellious cries. I allowed my mind to sabotage my body, and I became its hostage. I realize today that it was crying out, "Help! Slow down!" or, "You can't do this to me much longer!" or again, "Your pace is much too fast for me! I can't handle it! I'm hurting!" Instead of viewing these symptoms as my body's ways of warning me that something was not right and was dissuading me from that self-inflicted strain, I viewed them as being something that constituted a recuperating process and justified them as being the elements of a circumstance that would work itself out. My internal negotiating was embedded in a stronghold of obstinacy. This was a part of me that claimed a pernicious control and dictated some type of achievement. Loving my profession so much, and having renewed my rapport with the children, I lived and worked assiduously every single minute of every single day, of the next three years, just for my career. I was completely immersed in my work. I was drowning in it, and it was suffocating me. My supervisor had told me one late afternoon in closing a workshop, that a few of my colleagues had made the comment on my "sick" dedication. They had told him, "We love teaching, but we're not married to it like Diane is."

John had diligently tried to fill in as my life jacket. Loving me and knowing me the way nobody else did at that time, he quickly recognized the change in me and, patiently and tactfully, signaled it out. But no, I was fine…or so I thought. There was a war going on between my mind and my body. The pain was getting worse, and I was running out of fuel. Nevertheless, I always managed to defend it, to bargain with it, or at least tried to by telling myself, "Of course you'll feel tired; you work hard at what you do, and besides, you're not getting any younger."

I had thus entered the tunnel of denial. This denial stage has unrealistic power over you: you lie to yourself. I kept telling myself the pain would eventually go away or that it could not have been that intolerable. Maybe I just lacked sufferance or stamina. Maybe my capacity to endure was low. I was being totally stoic to the pain, and I finally felt good about myself. I was productive! I was bringing home a pay cheque. I was contributing my share to the household. I felt needed at my work. There was nothing wrong with what I was doing. I had relinquished all my anger. That in itself was a relief. The stage of bargaining had now begun. I would talk to myself. I would reason with myself, at least I though it was good reasoning. "You're not that tired! C'mon, you can do it! You can take it slower tomorrow, or maybe take a break on the weekend. You'll be fine." These lies were my bargaining tools. I had been playing head games. Only much later did I discover that chronic illness does not make deals, nor does it accept bribes.

Chapter VI: Sowing in Tears

"Foolish one, what you sow is not made alive unless it dies" (1 Corinthians 15:36).

From 1991 onward, my condition debilitated. My body was deteriorating. My health was impaired by overwork. Not only was I fighting it, but everything once taken for granted, such as getting dressed, preparing meals, washing and curling my hair, grocery shopping, making the bed, even something as simple as returning a telephone call, had become an arduous chore. My tolerance was flinching: the lights were too bright, the radio or television volume was too high, the murmur of people's voices in a restaurant created an uncomfortable and irritating buzzing in my ears. Everything was magnified. I wanted to lower the amplifier. Most of my nights were sleepless. If it wasn't the physical pain keeping me awake, it was the recurring nightmare of the accident. (As previously mentioned, I have no recollection of the actual impact. I only know what happened from reading the witnesses' reports: my body cartwheeling in the air, hitting the roof of the car, bouncing onto the trunk of the vehicle only to be thrown on to the roadway, crashing into a median and cracking my helmet.) How I regret reading those reports! Up until now, the images of that shocking evening of March 28, 1987, had been a blur. But now, six years later, the dreadful event had begun to flash and to unfold before my eyes. I was never able to fall back asleep after waking up in a heavy sweat from seemingly hearing the sound of screeching brakes and being blinded by the flashing of automobile headlights. I would go to bed drained from every type of expended energy and get up the next day feeling the same way, if not worse. My stamina was depleted. My body felt as if it had been in another accident; this time it had been run over by an eight-wheeler. Regardless of that strain, I was still putting in a full day's work as a Learning Resource teacher. I would have to make great efforts just to visit my family members and friends; and, once again, so many times I ruined

John's outings because I had to come home early. After a while, I was unable to follow conversations, which in normal times would interest me. I would be in a daze, and people around me noticed it. My concentration became even more limited than it had been. I noticed it more during the school's I.P.R.C. meetings; these once well-organized assemblies had now become stigmatized by my forgetfulness: missing a report or a form, not remembering a name or an important date relevant to the discussion at hand, etc. I found it difficult to focus my attention on anything else but the pain. I never knew what to expect. I was preoccupied with either a feeling of lightheadedness or a sad memory, or again with an oncoming anxiety attack. My speech was totally embarrassing! I would catch myself making word reversals such as saying, "I'm going there yesterday," instead of saying, "I'm going there tomorrow," or again, confusing words that started with the same letter such as, "magnetic" for "metallic," or "Rolodex" for "Rolex." Some of my students and acquaintances had noticed my mistakes and had graciously pointed them out. Many times, my mind would, for no reason, suddenly go blank in the middle of a sentence. It was as if an eraser was flying around, only to stop and rub out what I had planned to say. My neurotransmitters were out of whack! On other occasions when I tried to recall the name of a person or a place, I could only remember the first letter of the word. Attaching a name to a face or remembering my telephone number proved to be unsuccessful at times. There were also those moments when I would attempt to explain what was happening, and people who cared about me tried to be sympathetic by listening and would then express themselves by saying, "That's not like you, Diane. But we understand. We know how you must feel. It must be very frustrating for you." I would say to myself, "No, you don't! You have no idea! Please, don't tell me you know how I feel! You're not the ones going through this humiliation, so you couldn't possible know how I feel!"

I know today that, then, my anguish and embarrassment were self-inflicted. People were simply trying to comfort me, but since I have a tendency of being highly critical in general, I always thought of them judging me as being a boring and whining person. This feeling of inadequacy only heightened my suffering.

Not only did I have to cope with my pain, but also with John's. He also tried to deal with mine. People would have never known he was suffering. I envied him, being able to hide it. He was so good at pretending, until things grew a little too tense on the job. He was slowly building and filling his reservoir of anger. He would have never let on at work, but at home, he would express it, explode at times, in more ways than one. He would either become very quiet, even to the point of becoming introverted (which is completely out of character for John), or he would get very hyper and loud— a doctor Jekyll and Mr. Hyde personality! My need for peace and quiet was forever being attacked by these unruly demonstrations. We had been transformed into two plastic puppets, easily manipulated and controlled by each other, by our employer, by our families and friends, and by the justice system, which we still had to deal with over this pending legal matter, now eternising for six years.

Allow me to take a few lines to describe how the court systems can too often dictate people's lives. We had been hopeful that our legal claim would have at least been heard, if not settled, a couple of years after its onset. Unfortunately, three years following the accident, we were informed by both solicitors (one in Australia and one here in Ontario) that it would take a little longer, reason being that the accident had occurred overseas, and the defence lawyers wanted to wait longer to see how we would heal. For us, the case was plain and simple: we had been hit by an unlicensed drunk driver who had run a red light and was charged and convicted of those infractions. He had also left the scene of the accident, only to be chased a few blocks away and brought back by a good Samaritan taxi driver, while John and I laid on the road, both unconscious. We simply wanted to be compensated for our injuries and our lost wages. Was this not clear and fair enough? We wanted and needed some sort of finality to this ongoing nightmare and hoped to reconnect the best way we could, the last pieces of our puzzle called "life." However, for the judicial system, our case was much more intricate, so much so that it had been moved up to the Supreme Court of New South Wales. Meanwhile, we were both bounced back and forth to different doctors, specialists and treatment clinics, only to be prescribed each time with new and different medication, x-rays, and scans, and to be told what and what not to do. We had become their marionettes. We had lost control of our lives!

The ramifications of this lengthy encumbrance (now in its ninth year) locked us into an imprisoned lifestyle. How could we put this nightmare behind us when the defence lawyers kept requesting more and more medical reports, economists' analyses, and physiotherapists' evaluations? How could they expect us to put our anguish aside when we were constantly being reminded of it by the everyday pain or by the Australian facsimiles informing us with legal jargon of yet another postponement of a scheduled hearing, or again by everyone inquiring how our case was progressing. Comments such as, "You haven't settled yet?" or "Why is it taking so long?" or "How much longer will it take?" or again, "Is there nothing you can do to speed up matters?" or again, "You have been more than patient. Wouldn't it be to your advantage to take a stand with both law firms?" did not encourage us! If anything, they amplified our pain, our worries, and our hurt. That gray, heavy cloud seemed to forever linger over our heads, regardless of how hard we tried to disregard it. The word "manipulation" is defined as: "to control or play upon the artful, unfair, or insidious means, especially to one's own advantage." That's exactly what was happening with our situation: the solicitors were the controllers and getting richer, while John and I were the pawns and heading for the poor house.

When I started writing these last few lines, I had not planned on adding the following ones. Only after proof-reading them did I realize what they truly revealed. These latter thoughts had suddenly translated into Tao, thus the "unfolding." Yes, as the word "unfolding" is defined, this nine-year period became a panorama before my very eyes. I saw, and today strongly believe, that this length of time, painful as it was, served as an instrument for the cleansing and the healing of my soul, of my mind, and of my heart. Had someone told me nine years ago that my suffering was necessary in order for me to receive the gift, I would not have believed them. Quoting Helen Keller, "I thank God for my handicaps, for through them I found myself, my work, and my God," I learned that when we choose, and it is a choice, to drown in self-pity, we put limitations on our usefulness and service to mankind and to God. Today I know it was worth the price.

I must have been a hard one to recruit. However, God was patient with me. He wanted me on His side and kept knocking, but it took me those nine years before I decided to answer and to let His son, Jesus, into my life. Throughout the bickering back and forth with lawyers, I thought my only compensation would have been a cash settlement to help me put my life back on track. Little did I know that my greatest atonement would be the acquired consciousness and connectedness with Jesus, the Best Lawyer, and our Lord, the Best Judge, and the only Mediator of life's most important issues: love, faith, and power. But I'm getting ahead of my story.

Tension was building up between John and myself; the stress level was on the rise; the relationship was in an explosive state. The verbal abuse was increasing and reaching the stage of cruelty. Because the animosity was so intense, we thought keeping our distances would relieve some of the pressure and would mend things, but it only made them worse. What kind of relationship can two people in love have, when they are more or less forced to walk on egg shells and on their hearts? The facts were clear: I had become married to my career, and John was unhappy at work and at home. As a result of feeling this void, he started drinking heavily. It was now his turn to drown himself in a bottle of scotch. For the longest time, I had blamed myself for my first husband's addiction to alcohol. Was I failing again with my second partner? How weak we both had been! Our quest for courage and strength was not to be found in that kind of spirit. Little did we know then that we needed the infusion of a Holy Spirit. Ephesians 5:18 states: "Do not get drunk on wine, which leads to debauchery. Instead, be filled with the Spirit."

Had this been God's plan for us? During my teenage years, I would always get excited with my life's plans, and my mother, whom I considered a wise individual, having lived through many struggles and hardships herself, would often repeat to me this popular maxim that applied so well to my circumstance: "Diane, man proposes, but God disposes." I didn't know it at the time, but I do now. God had not planned this obstacle course in my life. My choices had predicted that. Nevertheless, God had a purpose in using it. What had been meant for something bad, He would turn around for something good. How well would I surmount the hurdles and get around the pylons?

During an April evening when everything started out fine, John's drinking got out of hand. His anger inundated the conversation. I left for school the next morning with a bruise on my arm and a heart broken by the words he spoke to me. It wasn't so much this pain that was bothering me now, but more so the idea of our once beautiful and gratifying relationship leading to this horror show. Ironically, I had just completed implementing an anti-violence campaign in my school. I drove to work almost in a daze with little regard to speed or to safety. I tried to make sense of what had happened, but I could not. Was I being tested by God again? I kept switching from heavy sobs to soft moans. If a knife wound causes a throbbing pain, then that's what I was feeling. I thought my head would explode, and my throat was on fire. Had this really happened, or was it simply a segment of this whole nightmare? Maybe when I wake up, it will be gone. For the first time since the Australian ordeal, I was able to present a superficial and deceptive facade to my colleagues and to my students. Keeping up a good front and appearing perfect was very important to me. One person, however, Pierre, the school's psychotherapist, who was always ready to read me, had warned me a few months back that my body wouldn't be able to handle the stress and the abuse I was putting it through for much longer. On this day he recognized my concealment and said, "Diane, you are the only one who is tightening the noose around your neck. You are strangling yourself. You are choking, and your body can't take it anymore. You had better start thinking of slowing down and doing something else. You are on the road to a complete physical and emotional disaster. Start thinking of Diane and the kind of relationship you have with John."

I kept trying to put it behind me, but it gnawed at me all day long. I felt so violated, so humiliated, so rejected, and so cheated! Things were never the same with John and me after that. Audre Lorde, in her book, *A Burst of Light*, explains: "Sometimes we cannot heal ourselves close to the very people from whom we draw strength and light; because they are the closest to the places and tastes and smells that go along with the pattern of living we are trying to rearrange." I knew I could never heal physically and emotionally by being a part of such a fragile, tense, violent, tempestuous, and destructive situation. It took all I had, nerve and energy-wise, to end the school year. The ongoing feeling of interminable fatigue, plus trying to cope with the physical pain, not to mention the end of a 10-year relationship, and the conviction of not living the right way, forced me to leave our small paradise on the lake. I found an apartment in my hometown near my school. I must have made forty trips moving my belongings in my small car. "God, are You with me, or are You just watching me?"

"Awake, O Lord! Why do you sleep? Rouse yourself! Do no reject 'me' forever. Why do you hide your face and forget 'my' misery and oppression?" (Psalm 44:23, 24)

My bible had told me that God is Love. Where was the love in this?

Chapter VII: Metamorphoses

A new school year was starting the week after I moved into my new place. It was now September 1993. I was looking forward to returning to school, as I always did. Two months off in the summer had always been too long for me. Prior to this past summer, I had organized and taught two summer school programs, and I had given some private tutoring sessions, but this time I was returning with more enthusiasm because I had accepted working with a team of individuals in the Special Education field. This "special" class focused on helping students who came from dysfunctional backgrounds. How ironic! My so-called life was dysfunctional, and I was helping them? Who was helping me?

I was now living alone, something I had never experienced before this time. In Teachers' College, I had a roommate, and even after my first husband had passed away, I had my two sons. I now enjoyed more time to myself: a time to think, to soul-search, and to meditate. My health was getting poorer, but I still strived on making things perfect in the classroom. Apart from the team of four colleagues I was working with, no one was helping me. I was doing my best to make the life of my students as pleasant and problem-free as possible. As I was meditating one night, I was faced with so many unanswered questions: Where would I end up? Would I always be alone? What about this chronic pain? Would it ever ease up? What was I to become?...No answers!

The people around me, mostly colleagues now, would inquire about my condition and my situation, some out of curiosity, and others with some genuine interest. They would listen attentively when I felt like sharing. I found myself in great need of spreading my wings, telling my story to everyone; it became a form of therapy for me. How good it was to do that, I don't know. Again, trying to console me, these compassionate and patient listeners would say, "That is really too bad. We can imagine how you must feel, but things can only get better for you. Try to keep your chin up. Time heals everything, Diane. You just have to be patient." That's not what I wanted or needed to hear. I wanted things to be better *now*! And as far as time was concerned, well, it had been nine years. One would think that Mr. Time had had his chance of doing his work. But looking back on this now, I learned that it was not in line with God's perfect timing, for when it is, He reveals it to us. I refuted their well-intended comments and explanations. I wanted to wail out, "Please, don't tell me you can imagine how I feel because you can't. You're not in my situation! Nobody knows how I feel but me! I'm here; I'm the one living in it! I'm the only one who knows what and how I feel!" This delusion had yet to be revealed. How I wished for a short moment these individuals could crawl into my body to know and to feel my anguish and my moroseness! I wanted to trade bodies so I could temporarily escape from my prison.

It had now become a ritual after school, for me to try and unwind in a steaming hot bubble bath, with hopes of bringing some relief to my tired, wretched, and aching body. It was on an overload! For the longest time I would lie there with my eyes closed, trying to relax, to numb the physical pain, wanting so desperately to forget and wishing to quietly evaporate into Lalla Land. I hated my life vehemently! I hated the unrelenting pain! I felt mortified! I was commiserating over my bad luck. Life had surely not dealt me a trump card! I remember the time when an "everything went wrong day" had been too much for me. As I rested in the bathtub, feeling so alone, trapped inside a body I hated, feeling cheated out of a good life, worried about tomorrow and scared of everything, I pictured myself floating around a galaxy of scenes and faces from my past. My life was laden with unfathomable complexities and laid in shambles before me. I had been through every emotion. I was wrung out! These frantic thoughts had driven me to place meticulously, every pill bottle on the edge of the tub. The labels were facing me; I had arranged them in a hierarchy, for I had planned on swallowing the milder ones first, then gradually reaching a crescendo with the strongest prescription. (Since no pill could kill the pain…then maybe I could). The anti-inflammatory pills were in first place, starting with the Ibuprofen, then the Naproxen, on with the Voltaren, to Idarac, closely followed by the Tylenol 3s. The Flexiril and the Paxil would then join this congregation inside my body, only to end the ceremony with Halcion, Amitriptyline and Diazepam. I had thought if this zealous protest did not kill me, then without a doubt, it would reach its climax and anaesthetize me for a few hours. An unexpected telephone call from my younger son Mike quickly ended my contemplation. He was inquiring on how I was feeling. Had I really wanted to commit suicide I would not have taken the time to answer my telephone. God works in mysterious ways! He wasn't finished with me yet!

That same evening, I threw all my pills into a bag, walked over to the building's garbage chute and dropped it with no hesitation whatsoever. Having come that close to ending my life with those invaders, I have since stayed away from any kind of prescribed medication that would only mask any kind of ailment. Didn't Molière write a long time ago, "Most men die of their remedies, not of their diseases."

I longed to share my feelings of guilt, failure, shame, anger and self-pity with someone who could and would understand them at face value. I hoped to find someone who could share my pain. I could not think of anyone who could identify with, relate to, or share these same mixed-up emotions. Sparks of fear were burning my insides. The aloneness I was experiencing left me torn, wounded and bleeding. I thought losing my mind would have been less painful. I thought the pain from my past had made me a survivor. I had successfully worked my way through degradation, physical abuse and sexual molestation from a private boarding school for girls, through shame from rape at the young age of fourteen, through grief from losing my dad to a heart attack, and through deep distress after the loss of my husband to cirrhosis of the liver. I was so used to being in control. (At least I thought I had been.) I had been brought up in a home and in a convent, wherein I had to be independent and self-reliant. I had to figure out a way of coming to terms with my crippling depression. It was not easy to let go of that control and submit to the control of the Lord, but it was the only way I could, once more, function successfully. It was the only way to survive. It was time to take a stand. I thought, "I can either 'go' through this, or I can 'grow' through it."

When I was in physiotherapy, I can recall coming across this profound statement in one of the magazines in the waiting room. "We are not responsible for our illnesses; we are responsible to them." I remember discussing in one of my psychology classes, the topic of personal choices; it explained that many of us have traumas that affect our personality, but the choices are our own. I had made a point of remembering that, and to this day, I repeat it to myself in my moments of weakness, in my times of backsliding, and of wanting to give up: "The choice is mine to own."

One October evening, I received a telephone call from John, who had just finished his night class at the local college. He asked me if he could come over for a coffee. Since we had to discuss a recent letter from our Australian solicitor regarding our claim for the accident, I agreed. We reviewed its content, only to be disappointed again by its agonizing delay. As we finished our coffee, we briefly inquired on how each one was doing. In saying good-night, I broke down crying. As he held me close to his chest, I cringed because the pain was so intense. His embrace felt like bolts of lightning shooting to various part of my body. Even my skin hurt! Still holding me, John said, "We'll get through this. Everything will work out. We'll be fine."

He cupped his hands around my face and gently kissed my forehead. This was the side of John I had not seen in two years. This was the John I knew and loved. He was being the optimist that he had always been before this bad dream. That's one of the reasons I had fallen in love with him. At that time, he was the one who gave me the buoyancy I needed to keep my head above the raging waters. In that sense, he was what I wasn't. From that time on, we started seeing each other again, and during the Christmas holiday, while entertaining both families, we decided to get back together and try once more. Our house on the lake went up for sale because the housework and the commuting to school had become too demanding on me. Our relationship was flourishing again. Our love was thriving, but toward a different goal. Our past experience had taught us a new set of values. Nevertheless, we still had our difficulties. John, at work, and I, steeped in poor health, along with increased financial woes: the house was not selling, and I had had my car stolen.

The anxiety attacks had surfaced again, causing me to faint, especially in the mornings before going to school. The stress level in the classroom was high, and my emotional state was being controlled by mysterious abysmal powers, as panic would emerge into frenzy. This had become an ever-increasing problem, and more so now, because I had developed a driving phobia. Not only did I worry or feel that someone was going to hit me while driving, but now I was apprehensive of either passing out while driving or, worse yet, in front of my students. If only I had known the Word then, I could have relied on this scripture from Isaiah 41:9-10: "Do not fear, for I am with you; do not be dismayed, for I am your God. I will strengthen you and help you; I will uphold you with my righteous right hand."

My nights remained sleepless. I felt like a ship sailing off to nowhere. I had allowed anxiety and worry to re-enter the port and take over my ship. These feelings were drilling holes in my hull. My vessel was sinking, and I felt that Jesus had fallen asleep on my boat. The pain was insufferable. I was experiencing strong palpitations. My days of absenteeism from school were occurring frequently. My depression was rapidly intensifying. I was a mess again!

The visit to my doctor in February 1994 was the culmination of all my disappointments. Having been diagnosed in early September with the chronic fatigue syndrome, and because of my unbalanced frame of mind, I was ordered to take a complete break from school until the spring holidays. Exhaustion is the hallmark of this condition. Naturally I cried. This was still another unexpected catastrophe. He said, "You don't have any other choice, Diane. You need a complete rest. I know it's hard for you to accept this. I know how you feel, but there is no other way." One would think that the doctor knows how the patient feels, but I still felt like saying, "No, you don't know how I feel. You don't feel like I do. You're not inside my body. You're not inside my head. You couldn't know! Please, don't tell me you know and understand how and what I feel. Teaching is the only good thing that keeps me going right now, and you're taking it away from me!"

I went home and told John, who wasn't too surprised by the news. The next day, I tried to convince myself that my predicament wasn't that bad. I had one month to rest, to restore anew the cells in my body, to build up my strength, and to start restructuring my thinking process into positive patterns. Tall order! It was not an easy assignment to undertake. I tried so hard. I was determined to do it. I made myself believe that the pain, which was now controlling my entire body, was not that limiting. I wasn't that tired; my depression would lift; I would return to school in no time. My therapist had once told me that healing goes through its own season. I believed that a new season would begin for me, and I would be ready to spring up. I would be blooming again alongside the day lilies. Everything would be coming alive once more after a long, harsh winter, including me.

Such was not the case. My doctor did not prescribe my return to teaching, but was rather forced into referring me to a rheumatologist. In April 1994, I reached the plateau of my fate. I was diagnosed as having a condition called fibromyalgia. I had never heard the word before this time. The specialist explained to me and to John that it was a condition often caused by a trauma to the body through surgery or by an accident; it can sometime start with an illness like influenza, and in some people, it may develop after a sudden hormonal change, such as occurs with a hysterectomy after the birth of a child, or again, the symptoms may begin to appear for no reason at all. He went on to explain that the condition is characterized by diffuse muscular

49

aching associated with sleep disorder, headaches, and excessive fatigue; other related symptoms that I also had were increased pain perception, depression, abnormal muscle spasms, forgetfulness, inability to concentrate, dizziness, sensitivity to heat and cold, hair loss, difficulty swallowing, and panic attacks, only to name a few. I was fortunate, if one can say that, not to have the other related symptoms. As he was describing how this condition affected an individual (more often women than men), it made so much sense to me now. This pain, these feelings…they were all real! They weren't all in my head! It wasn't my imagination! It wasn't due to my lack of tolerance! I wasn't exaggerating! Yes, it was true that I was tired! Yes, it was true that my skin hurt! Yes, it was true that I felt depressed! Yes, it was true that I couldn't sleep! And yes, it was true that I was hurting!

I should not have felt happy or relieved when he announced what I had, but in a strange sort of way, I was. I even felt exultant, because now I finally knew why I had felt this agony for so many years! I could finally attach a name to this misery. I had fibromyalgia! Well now, I thought, he'll prescribe some medication (even though I feared it because of my close call experience with it), and in no time I'll be functional again. I realized and accepted that I was, and would remain partly limited in a sense, due to the injuries sustained in the accident. But that was okay. I had somehow learned to cope with those for all those years. Now I had to accept and learn to deal with this other new affliction.

Another surprise was in store for me. He told me there was no cure for fibromyalgia and no magic pill. He did reassure me, or at least tried to, by informing me that an aerobic program might be conducive to my well-being. He asked me if I was interested in participating in such a program. The treatment, he went on to explain, also had components of pain management. He didn't seem to think at the time that my previous accident injuries would interfere with the exercises. Wanting so much to feel better, I agreed.

As we drove home, I kept to myself. I tried to keep a positive perspective. I was almost calm. I finally knew what was wrong with me. I felt myself slowly moving away from the panic button. The vibration was reduced. Throughout my many meditative readings, I learned that a re-framing of the mind is possible. All this time (now close to eight years), I had allowed my negative emotions to dim my sight and to warp my vision. God can give us new hopes, but we need to place all of our negative feelings and thoughts on the Cross. That was my plan. I suddenly understood why the symbol of spiritual awakening is the death of Jesus on the cross. One has to die to self in order to live!

I had mixed emotions: I was feeling melancholy after being told there was no cure for my condition, but on the other hand feeling exuberant because of the strong possibility of returning to work after the intended physiotherapy 10-week program. Two months passed before I was called by the rehabilitation center, and I was concerned about the delay. I had it all figured out: I would give the program all I had for the months of July and August, and I would be ready to return to teaching in September. I was being positive. I was putting every dismal thought behind me. During the drive to the treatment center that first day, July 7 (which, by the way, took all my courage to drive there because of my driving phobia), I said to myself, "You are going to be the best one in the group. You will give it your all, and you will be the best that you can be." I walked in there, feeling so confident. I wanted to be a ray of sunshine, regardless of the pain in my body. Once again, I yearned to be referred as a breath of fresh air, as I had been called in Australia. On the questionnaire that I was asked to answer, one of the questions was, "What do you expect to gain from this program?" I wrote, "I want to help myself and help others suffering from this syndrome." On the first morning, I felt reassured about the program. I was introduced to the other members of the support group, and it didn't take too long for me to feel understood by them. Everyone in the group had been diagnosed as suffering from fibromyalgia; therefore, everyone was able to identify with and relate to what and how the other one was feeling. Talking about the pain, our frustrations with it, sifting through our feelings, sorting out our inner conflicts—all of the issues became an important release of bottled-up emotions for all of us. This venting was already helping me in dissolving my pent-up destructive feelings.

The first few weeks didn't bother me too much, but the commuting back and forth to the center four mornings a week, and being there from 9 o'clock till noon, was very draining. The conversation I held with myself, reasoning every move during the drive, became pretty nerve-racking. The following week, however, my whole body felt like it had been run over by a bulldozer. The therapists reassured me by informing me that it was perfectly normal because I was using muscles that had been more or less dormant for quite a while and that the stiffness would gradually be reduced, but not totally eliminated. It made so much sense at the time; I wanted to believe it so much, and because my fixation was to be the best "patient" in the group, I was pushing myself to the extremes. The physiotherapists had explained to the group that inactivity could lead to more problems. Having lived in the throes of constant pain, I concluded that if I kept myself active, I would heal quicker. I completely denied again what my old injuries were signaling. Once during one of our education classes, the social worker leading the discussion was listening to the group members explaining and sharing how they felt. One was having severe headaches; another was not sleeping; another said she was always crying; still another expressing his anger toward this impairment that kept him from working; and I was sharing the difficulties that this condition was causing in my relationship with John and with some members of both families. They had grown more or less tired and apathetic to my discomfort. Individuals with this syndrome need to have some quiet time when they can rest and internalize, which in turn can, at times, make them become rigid and appear to be demanding in their ways. They resist intervention, they don't like to be pitied, and they take offense easily. Family members and friends often think that the "sick" person lacks will power, does not want to accommodate, tends to be melodramatic, and has turned into an attention-seeker. More often than not, the person looks well. As a result of this ignorance and misunderstanding of the syndrome, the "well" individuals often label the victims of this condition as "chronic complainers," "whiners," or "control freaks" for appearing to want things done their way. Thus, the sufferers do not receive the support and the encouragement they need. Instead, they are expected by family members, insurance companies, and employers, to answer to the demands of everyday living and to jump back into the helter-skelter of life as soon as possible. On hearing our complaints, the group leader added, "Listen. That's why you're all here. We will help you learn how to cope with these problems. We understand. We know how you feel." There was that false statement again, "*We know how you feel!*" which triggered in me a volcano of resentment. I was having one of my "hell" days that morning, and had been for the past few. I exploded, "How can you say that, Bonnie? There is no way you could know how we feel. Do you have this kind of pain and frustration? You don't, because you don't have this fibromyalgia condition. So please don't say you know how we feel. Sure, you read about this condition in the literature, and you must attend some workshops and health seminars where the doctors brief you on its symptoms and limitations, but that's all. You don't have a clue of what the pain is like!" I didn't make the next session. I was still too upset and was ashamed of my exaggerated outburst.

My silent wish to exit this life was resurfacing again. This time the memory of my deceased husband drifted into my mind, and while kneeling in front of his grave, I tried to understand the mystery of death. I had come to the cemetery many times before desperately trying, somehow, some way, to communicate with Claude, asking his advice regarding our two sons. But now, after 13 years of widowhood, I missed him. He had been my first love. We had planned a large family and had intended to grow old together. But this day, I was coming for myself. What kind of relationship can one have with the dead? Somehow I longed to be close to him again. I wanted to join him. I wanted to die! I knew there was room in there for me by his side, as I had purchased a double plot at the time of his death. How comforting it would be to escape into that underground refuge, at least for a short while! Maybe his existence in another realm would allow and enable him to give me some answers or just help me to see things more clearly. The more I tried to analyse it, the more confused I became.

Chapter VIII: Satori:
The Awakening

Long before the treatment program, I had enrolled in a weekend of Inner Healing and Well-Being. It was expensive, but it was worth every penny. I was able to redirect my grief and my anger toward this alien that had invaded my body and had robbed it of its privacy and self-worth. That's what this illness had become: a foreign thing. All this time, being now well over seven years, the condition had taken the role of an incubus. During that weekend, I cried over "it"; I threw things at "it"; I swore at "it"; I hit and punched "it." I was purging myself of this "beast." It turned out that these so-called "fits" or "temper tantrums" resulted in my personal renunciation of the close association I had with "it." A couple of days following this "dramatic" surrender, it suddenly came to me to sit down and write "it" a letter.

Dear Fibromyalgia,

A little over seven years ago, you came into my body. Many things have changed since that time. Both you and I don't know why we met, but we're here together now. I hate the pain and the agony you cause. Why do you have to do this to me? What did I ever do to make you angry with me and want to hurt me? Sometimes I get angry at you, but right now I'm not; I'm sad and confused. I have so many unanswered questions about your being. You have invaded my entire body, and it feels like you only want to destroy me. Maybe if we listen to each other, we can find a way to cope together and exist in peace. Suffice to say, I do not like the pain I'm going through with you, and I do not like the suffering you're making me endure physically, mentally, and emotionally. I know you probably will never go away completely, but I pray daily. I don't like to see my loved ones' helplessness toward you. You hide in my body; you never show yourself to them. They don't know you; they have never met you. They don't understand what you are about.

I know the power of the mind is bigger than you. It does, and it will make a difference. Now I have to learn to alter my life in some positive ways. I have to learn to take care of myself first. I know my mind is much more powerful than you; therefore, I will not let you win, but I do know that I have to work with you. We will get through this together.

Fibromyalgia, this is my promise to you. I do not give you the control over me; I give it to God!

A hopeful victim, Diane

That same evening I asked John to read my letter. After doing so, his comment was, "Very powerful!" (John had always encouraged me to write; he believed I could do it.) Expressing my feelings on paper was such a release. During my stay in Australia, I read about the aboriginal beliefs, and one of them was that being sick can be an experience that cleanses and purifies, and it is through this trial that the suffering person is able to receive a revelation of destiny and spirituality. These suppressed emotions were no longer imprisoned in the realm of abstraction. The simple yet difficult exercise of writing them down had made them come to life and had made them real to labor with. It became a gateway to my healing. I felt I had no more room left in my heart for these stumbling blocks. That's when I realized that I had made way through all of the five stages of acceptance:

Denial: In the beginning, I tried to ignore the pain.
Anger: I became consumed with rage.
Depression: I allowed total discouragement to overpower me.
Bargaining: I tried to make deals with my condition.
Acceptance: I decided to let go of all my negative emotions.

Yes, I had reached the final stage of accepting this plague. I wouldn't give up, and I would make it. I then realized that putting everything behind me, even finding it in my heart to forgive the drunk driver who had inflicted the pain, was one of my first steps toward recovery. Hence, the biblical principle, "When one forgives, one finds God's grace." It took me a long time, but I learned to recognize the "enemy" as an agent for my own enlightenment. By forgiving that young man, I was able to achieve my own freedom. The biblical injunction from the Lord's Prayer has now taken a new meaning: "…forgive us our trespasses as we forgive those who trespass against us."

I found myself in urgency of settling a score by making amends with certain individuals. After 14 years of not speaking to three sisters-in-law, I found the courage and the strength to reach out to them, humbling myself and asking their forgiveness. During Passover week, on Holy Saturday, I apologized for my wrongdoing and gratefully accepted forgiveness from one of my colleagues to whom I had not spoken to for years. I sensed I was entering the realm of grace. I had made up my mind that, not if, but when I learn and am able to cope with this mysterious pain, I would know how to listen, to understand, to care for, and to love others who are hurting. I was actually starting to praise God for using my suffering to bring me to this place. The pain became a part of the happiness. Through it all, I was developing a new kind of relationship with God. I knew that amidst my angst and my oppression, something good would come of it. It was a time for growing. I felt and I believed that God was working in me. It was His means to refine me. It was at that moment that I attained an awareness of divine connection. I heard His voice within me. What an appropriate time to finish reading the book, *Let Go, and Let God*, by A.E. Cliffe. Is it not true that every exit is but an entrance to somewhere else?

Nevertheless, life would be throwing me more curves and detours! When I arrived at the center the next day after my Inner Healing and Well-Being weekend, the group noticed the change in me right away. They said, "Diane, you look rested. You must have had a good weekend. Even your voice sounds different. What happened? Tell us about it." I briefly explained the format of the sessions; then I asked the social director in charge if I could share with the group the letter I had written to Fibromyalgia. When I finished reading it, I looked up only to find some members crying, others with their heads down, and the rest with a tear in their eyes. I was surprised by this kind of reaction, and I suddenly felt uncomfortable. I said, "I didn't expect my sharing to have this sort of impact on you. I didn't want to upset anyone. I'm sorry." Marilyn, said, crying, "That is so touching." Nena added, "A lot of feeling in there." Nassim, another worker, said, "That's very moving, Diane." Then Bonnie, our group leader, asked me if she could make photocopies of the letter to hand out to the group. I hesitated and thought. I had poured out my heart to this ailing condition, and I felt this unveiling of my thoughts and feelings belonged to me. I expressed that another fellow sufferer may feel differently toward this syndrome, so I declined. I wasn't comfortable with the idea of having my letter exploited that way, but I did suggest to the participants to find their own style, their own mode of expression in addressing their pain and suffering. Writing to "It," or even drawing or painting "It" could become an exercise of relief. Whichever method they chose to confront "It" could also possibly help them in the same way that writing to "It" had helped me.

I was filled with passion and vigor during the next few days after my communication with the "disease," but this energy, again, lasted that: a few days. The pain was becoming increasingly more unendurable. My injured hip had again started acting up. I was once more walking with a limp. My depression was overtaking me again; I was always crying. John was finding it more and more intolerable to deal with me. His patience was running out; anger was setting in. One night he said, without castigation, "Crying will only make it worse. I know how you feel; I have pain too. There's nothing I can do for you. If there is, please tell me." I became so enraged; there was acid in my voice. My reply was nefarious. I screeched out, "Don't tell me you know how I feel! If you want to know how I feel, just walk in my shoes. You don't know how I feel because you don't have my pain. At least you can go to work three days a week and function." I realized then that, not only had I become envious of him because he could work and I couldn't, but I had also turned into a jealous person. The questions to myself were tinged with bitterness. Why was it that he could work and I couldn't? We had been in the same accident together. What had I done to deserve this? I had read somewhere that one of the spiritual laws is that for every harmful act committed, one must pay the price of suffering. Was I that bad of a person? What do I have to do? How can I get God to rescue me? I was seeing myself as a sacrificial lamb. Was I another Job that God was using as an example to others? I was able to relate to Tolstoy's feeling, "There have been times when I felt I was becoming the bearer of God's will."

Our relationship was spiraling downward. John had grown into a petulant human being, and I, an invalid. The silent treatment and the avoidance of each other's presence in the room had once more gained control of our lives. These old behavior patterns were escalating anew. The air throbbed with gloom. John would shun this hostile environment by escaping to the marina to drown himself into his small charter fishing business, either by going out to sea or sitting on the boat with one too many scotches. All that time, I believed I was with God. Not so! Satan was after me, and he was succeeding. I hit bottom! I lived in constant fear of the future! I was desperate for answers. My voracious curiosity led me to an intense search for solutions to my problems in all kinds of "how to" and "self-help" books written on illness and relationships, and to explore many terrains of spiritual healing. I probed everything I could find on these topics because I wanted to make sense of them. I had exhausted all natural resources. I didn't understand what was happening to my body. I wanted to know what it needed.

One afternoon while sitting in the reference department of our local library, I was reading an article by Jung on Alchemical Studies, when the answer to my zillion questions jumped right out at me. The author stated, "When God is not acknowledged, egomania develops, and out of this mania comes sickness." There was my answer! God! It was clear to me now that the many books I had read had indeed informed me, but only His Word could transform me. I needed a supernatural touch, but I felt that nothing was moving. I was desperately trying to commune with God again: "God, where are You? Are you testing me?" I felt disconnected from everyone and everything!

I will never forget one incident at the center when I became overwhelmed with the pain. What happened was such a frightening moment! I felt like a helpless prey to a force beyond my control. The pain had become my master; it was now controlling me. I had, once more, become enslaved by its power. My body felt like a block of concrete; I could not move! My whole body was spasmodic! My head felt like a football being kicked around back and forth. I could not stop crying. I was panicking. My breathing became labored. I was hyperventilating. The therapists and workers had to page the resident doctor. Before considering using the small oxygen cylinder he had brought with him, he had me take deep breaths into a paper bag. The room was spinning faster and faster, but I didn't lose consciousness. I slowly calmed down. My breathing returned to normal. It had been a terrifying twenty minutes.

That night before retiring, I talked to God. Actually, I was imploring Him, "God, where are You when it hurts? Are You not the Great Physician, the Healer Who brings comfort to His children? Please God, help me get through this." Had Jesus not implored God, "My Father, if it be possible may this cup be taken from me" (Matthew 26:39)? This thought permeated every cell of my aching and weary body. It seemed the closer I grew to God, the farther He was. Only now do I know that this was a part of His plan to draw me to a closer, stronger, and more divine level with Him.

59

One evening after dinner, I went for my regular 25-minute walk, pushing myself into lighter aerobics, hoping it would heal me quicker. Each day, each hour, each minute, I was deciding between the crucifixion and the resurrection. The thieves were nailed to the crosses next to Jesus; I was nailed to this life of disappointments and suffering. Was my cross also next to Jesus? What had happened to the "acceptance" stage I thought I had reached? Was I slowly dying, or would I be able to rise over this? Jesus had resurrected Lazarus; was He willing to do the same for me?

I know today what I needed then, more than aerobics, was spiritual calisthenics. But as I walked, I became more and more despondent. Every passing tree became a station of the Cross. I was losing ground. My whole world was out of sync. My mind was racing. Why me? Did I deserve this? Was I was being punished for my sins? Was I being cursed? If there was no cure for the way I was feeling, why go on? I'm a burden to myself; John had told me that I was his biggest problem; and I had become a constant worry to my sons. I didn't have my health. I was locked in a dungeon of frustration. I couldn't sleep. I hurt all over. I was angry because I couldn't do the things I used to do, and I was envious of those who could. I had lost my passion for everything. My condition did not allow me to work. I was not bringing in any money to support the household. I felt guilty for so many things. (I had read somewhere that guilt is the ego's orgasm). I loathed my empty life. I was coming apart at the seams. I was a prisoner of a self-abnegation! I was totally enmeshed in my conflicts. My thinking was becoming toxic. These amorphous meanderings of my mind…were they a sign that I was falling apart? Were these thoughts telling me that I had had it?

I had ruminated over these same questions so many times. My tormented thoughts were running amok; my emotions were drifting without restraint. I didn't want to have a role to play in this drama called "Life." How does one eradicate oneself from a world of pain? I wanted my own private exodus! What about the question of ending it all? *Suicide*, I thought.

I was flogging myself again. A dense fog shrouded my brain. I was groveling in the mud of delusion. I was lost in a vacant reverie. I had bottomed out! Satan had me in his vise-like grip! I either had to be under his spell, in a trance, or in a state of lunacy, because I found myself mesmerized, standing catatonic-like on an abandoned bridge overlooking a canal, staring at the water. I felt disaster approaching me. Since I feared water and can't swim, what a perfect opportunity to end all of my problems and to take a load off of my loved ones.

Earlier on, I had asked God where He was. Well, He was with me then, He had to be, because the faces of my two sons came into focus through the rippling waters, and that's one of the reasons I stopped myself from jumping in. The other one was the invisible hand I felt on my shoulders. The devil had had his hands on me, but God was pulling me back. I realized, with the grace and the mercy of God, that ending my life was not the answer for me, or for anyone else for that matter. The idea of ending one's life is a lie from Satan because suicide is an act of vanity, selfishness, and cowardice. I felt there was no way to resign myself from this dilemma. I knew God was working overtime with me, but I still felt trapped inside a tightly-sealed box. I craved to be the Jack-in-the box who could pop out and surprise everyone. There had to be a solution to all of this. As a teacher working at one time with gifted students, I would be the one teaching the group various ways on how to come up with creative problem-solving techniques. Why could I not apply those same strategies to my existing crisis? My problem here was somewhat different. I couldn't find a solution. The Good Book had told me that God loves us, and He never abandons us. But where was He now? Why was He being so silent? He wasn't answering my plaintive calls. Was He too busy, or was He taking care of someone else? When would it be my turn? My confidence index was around the zero mark. Through this affliction, I have now learned that when our world is dark and we can't seem to be able to help ourselves and nobody else can, God can, and will, if we ask Him. In my times when I felt trapped, hurt and discouraged, He knew it. My cries were the beacons that brought Him to my side. He had heard the faintest of my cries for His help.

Soon after this accidental disclosure to one of the social workers at the treatment center (I had not told of this incident to anyone), my doctor, along with the therapists and the working team, agreed that the program was too much for me, the reason being that my entire situation was overflowing with too many unresolved issues for me to handle all at once. Being in treatment for Fibromyalgia was an added-on stress that I just couldn't deal with at this time. I had enough on my plate. I was discharged from the program one month before its final day. My objective of being the best patient in the group had turned into a joke. I had failed before everyone. Typical of a teacher, I was berating my performance. And what about becoming my bubbly "old self" again and hoping to help others? Had this become a lie too? I didn't know who I was, and I was too exhausted to find out.

The week following, my discharge found me still at the center, not in body, but in spirit. I kept thinking of what the group was doing around the 9:45 period, during the break, and again at 10:45 a.m. I wanted to be there; I wanted to feel better; I wanted to heal. During the first week away from the treatments, I received a telephone call from one of my cousins, informing me that one of our uncles had just passed away with cancer. Wanting to represent my family (my mother had moved to another province, my sister lived out of town, and since the death of our father, my brother couldn't handle being in a funeral home), I made an effort of going to pay my respects. For a short moment, my wish and need for peace and quiet was granted. I was losing myself in thought. I stared at my uncle lying there on that soft satin pillow and drifted. How comfortable he must be! No more pain...no more coping...no more efforts to make the best of it. I yearned for that exhilarating feeling of being at peace.

The sound of soft music brought me back to reality. How deranged my thoughts were! Wanting to, or even entertaining the morbid idea of exchanging places with a person in a coffin, was certainly not healthy. Would I ever be able to think of other things besides dying? I knew I was alive, but I wasn't living! I had to take hold of my senses and pull myself, once and for all, out of this paralysing cave of despair. This pit surely felt like a grave, but I knew it wasn't. I kept telling myself, "Get out there and join the rest in the Land of the Living."

I must admit, however, that three weeks after this unwholesome scene, the heaviness started to lift. My cries to God and my friends' prayers for me were being answered. My miracle was slowly being shaped. I felt different. I was getting back some strength. The pain was not as acute as it had been. I was resting a little better. I was following the helpful hints from a sleep disorder seminar I had attended at the center: sleeping on an egg-crate mattress to cushion my sensitive muscles and drinking hot milk and eating a few soda crackers before retiring. My thoughts became more positive. I wasn't crying as much. All along, I had placed total blame on my condition, and I had clung to the pain. Now I knew that my emotions and my frame of mind had a heavy impact on my struggle with it. This Indian quote from a reading during a philosophy course elective I had taken a while back comes to mind: "If you want to know what your thoughts were like yesterday, look at your body today. If you want to know what your body will be like tomorrow, look at your thoughts today." It applied perfectly to my circumstance.

The "have to's" weren't as numerous now, and they had lost their importance. I had learned, unwillingly that is, to unlearn old habits, to pace myself according to the kind of day I was having. I had been cursed with perfectionism, only to become enamored with it when illness had forced me to accept a moderate quality. I was faced with accepting a new doctrine, one of dualism: the good along with the bad, the strong and the weak, both attainment and shortcoming, along with the organization and disorder. I could no longer aspire to a level of high achievement. Each morning was unpredictable. I was now experiencing three kinds of days: "hell" days (can't get out of bed days), "okay" days (can do certain things days), and "good" days (can almost function like a normal person despite the pain days). I actually kept hoping, and I still do, of maybe having a "great" day. 2 Chronicles 15:7 often comes to mind: "...'I must' be strong and 'must' not give up, for there is reward for 'my' work." I just had to ask God to refine and to increase my faith in Him, to restore my soul, and to teach me humility and meekness.

In today's society, there is much injustice. Evil doings are very much alive and rampant. Unfortunately, life here on earth is like that. Those are the true facts of life. Our world is ruled by two powers: good and evil. Robert H. Schuller counsels us not "to confuse that facts of life with the acts of God." He states that "the acts of God can redeem the facts of life," but we have to hold on to the belief that our Lord is always by our side to see us through every trial. He will never force truth on anyone, but He does hear the cries of those who are searching for it. He did say, "Ask and you will receive, and your joy will be complete" (John 16:24). Through the journey of despair, God has helped me say to others, "I know what you're going through; I've been there."

Chapter IX: The Seed Is Sprouting

As I look back now, I know that I started working toward my victory the day I invited and accepted Jesus into my heart, and when I made up my mind to write about the experience that led me to the miracle. I always knew I had God in my life; I knew about Him, His story, but I was never told that one could know Him personally. In John 14:6, Jesus said to his disciples, "I am the way and the truth and the life. No one comes to the Father except through me."

Today, I have a close, personal relationship with God, through His Son, Jesus Christ. He is real, He is benevolent, He is glorious, He is omnipotent, He is precious, and He is my best friend. I didn't know at the time when I read Audre Lorde's advice in her book, *A Burst of Light*, "Find some particular thing your soul craves for nourishment, and do it," that writing about this miracle would help to save mine. He can and He does use our struggles, our battles, our pain to bring about His glory in us.

I first started out by wanting to express my feelings as a form of self-therapy. As everyone around me had grown tired of listening to my story, I was led to put my emotions on paper. The word "purging" is the best one that comes to mind to describe what I was living. Even though I had much difficulty concentrating and organizing my thoughts, I found myself looking forward to those times when I could sit down and write. I sensed that Someone was listening. I was recapturing my self-worth and discovered that I was gradually reconciling myself with this dilemma. Writing was quelling the pain. The times when I was able to disregard, and sometimes even forget the pain, were the hours I spent writing about it. When I felt too much discomfort sitting at the dining room table, I would sit in bed, resting against my heating pad and writing at my small breakfast table. The idea of reliving my story on paper enabled me to create from my problems, something that became beautiful. Since I could not return to my teaching duties on that first day of the new school term after the Labor Day weekend, I decided that my daily curriculum would now revolve around my writing tablet and my computer. I was faced with the choices of either accepting to live without my career or not living at all. My 35-year addiction to working with young people needed to be broken. The author of *Why Me, Why This, Why Now?* explains the aftermath of an addiction through these words she herself borrowed from a friend: "An addiction offers a person an opportunity to clean up a great deal of karma in one lifetime. But it's always a gamble, because recovery requires such a complete and constant surrender of the personal will to a Higher Power."

I chose life. I no longer felt constricted. I felt free and uplifted. I felt cleansed with His Spirit. Somehow I sensed a surge of a new and different kind of energy. Each writing session began with a personal prayer from my heart. My thoughts coalesced into words; they were coming into place and were flowing on paper. I asked God to give me the grace, the strength, and the boldness to pull myself from the self-imposed shackles I had been chained to, and out of the swamp I had been stuck in for the longest time. I had once broken away from moral moorings and had found myself in the center of a storm. I was so tired of being in polluted, stagnant, disease-infested stinking waters. I needed to be in cool and refreshing water.

"Save me, O God, for the waters have come up to my neck.
I sink in the miry depths where there is no foothold.
I have come into the deep waters;
The flood engulfs me.
I am worn out calling for help; my throat is parched" (Psalm 69:1-3).

I wanted to go upstream to spawn. I wanted life! I wanted newness! Since God is the Specialist of New Beginnings, He was guiding me through my treacherous course. He was showing me the way to my new emergence.

Marc, the pastor of the church I attend, had once told me that God delights in mending broken people and making them whole. He has a special adhesive to glue back together all the broken pieces of our heart, our spirit, and our body. This year was to be mine with the Lord. It would be a year of joy in which my listening to, and my reading of His word would increase, and with this increase, my inner peace would grow. This essential gift in my attitude toward my affliction has changed its power over my body and my mind, because this authentic power can only come from within our soul.

For the last seven years, but more so in the last six months, I had unsuccessfully searched for answers. My "false" gods had been my career, my expensive clothes, my obsession and compulsion with vanity, along with making good money: all things I had competed with, and which had become a hindrance to my relationship with Him. Thomas à Kempis, author of *Imitation of Christ*, states, "If you seek your Lord Jesus in all things, you will truly find Him, but if you seek yourself, you will find yourself and that will be to your own great loss." Even though these last few years have been the worst ones of my life, I truly have to say that they have been the most revealing and enriching ones. I needed a change, I deserved a change, and change was due. Throughout this trial of faith and patience, I had kept asking myself, "Why?" But now the "why?" and even the "why me?" turned into "why not?" What did become valuable, but more so of paramount significance, was knowing and believing that God loved me and accepted me the way I was. But I sensed and knew that His love would change me and heal me.

The decision to cleanse myself of all my sombre feelings was a revelation from God. The times of despair, desolation, and failure have been vanquished and have transpired into the seeds of revelation: the empowering emotions of love, faith, and power. I came to accept that nothing other than knowledge of and trust in my Lord Jesus Christ could ease the pain of my past. The old maxim applies: "When the student is ready, the Teacher appears." Paradoxically, my role was reversed; I was no longer the teacher, but became the student, and an attentive one at that. The Good Book has now become the learning manual, and God is the Professor. I had failed my previous course, but now, I was determined to graduate with honors and, as a result, would be promoted to a higher level.

In one of my spiritual readings, it explained that failure isn't the end but rather the beginning of our experience of God's restoration. This sentence from a great preacher in our church sticks in my mind: "Adversity can be a roadway to destruction or a pathway to promotion." I came to cultivate a more intense and deeper contact with my Inner Guide. The more I connected with my own insides, the more I became aligned with my spiritual side. I had to find the part of His Image that was inside of me; I was trying to make a deeper connection with myself. I had finally answered His knock at the door of my heart, heard His voice, and decided to follow Him. Following someone requires knowing the person's character, the plans he has, and how he plans to carry them out. I was prepared to allow Him to reshape me in what He wanted me to be. I know now that it's in His plan for me to lend a hand, as well as an ear, to all those who are suffering and floundering like I was. In doing so, I would heal. The workbook, *A Course in Miracles*, states it clearly: "…healing evolves replacing fear with love." It became apparent to me that love was the arena for my growth and the only avenue for me to follow, but I knew that I could not do it alone. I had tried many times before, and I had failed each time. The message came to me again in this sentence from the same book. What a powerful message it was when I first read it, and it remains still today: "Health is the beginning of the proper perspective of life under the guidance of one Teacher Who knows what life is, being the voice of Life itself."

Another unsuccessful search I had to accept during my most trying times was not finding a person who had been through the same problems and who had been victorious. My defeat compelled me to reach out. It had been so difficult for me to find someone who had the compassion to listen and to help me vacuum some of my dark and heavy feelings. However, I managed to find that "good ear" in my friends, Pauline, Chris, Lana, Louise, and Lynda. They became my caring and attentive, not to mention very patient listeners, whom God had placed as messengers and laborers on my path. The ruts on my bumpy road were slowly being filled with my friends' advice and prayers. Through them, He was speaking, He was helping me, and He was showing me His love and how to love. Did He not create us for the sole purpose of loving and being loved? I soon discovered that love is not so much a feeling, but more of an attitude and an action. I was now enjoying a somewhat ethereal presence inside me. Once again, I felt His anointing. It was there for me, and all I had to do was to grab and hold on to it. This is where I'm at today.

In another one of my readings, this old aphorism remains indelible in my mind: "Getting down on your knees is a method of getting back on your feet." I did just that, and my shell of despair was broken. Today I consider myself a free spirit, a conqueror. My life has equilibrium. I am celebrating! I value life! My soul is replenished with a new kind of awe and marvel at this new path in my life. I always knew that God was real, but today, when I'm asked if I believe in God, I shock people and enjoy their reaction when I answer with Jung's statement, "No, I do not. I KNOW there is God." I learned to resist the many arguments of those around me who question the trustworthiness of God. It is also said that "When people cease to believe in God, they don't believe in nothing, they believe in anything" (G. K. Chesterton).

It is through this frightful labyrinthian journey, hindered by the many pitfalls and the many mine fields planted on my path, that I discovered that the Good Lord has waited all along for the opportunity to help me, and all I had to do was to ease up and give Him some space. He was giving me a second chance to observe what I had neglected: life in His Word.

By giving Him that opportunity, I learned that it didn't mean that I was abandoning my responsibility, nor was I giving up. Formerly, I had querulously pled my difficulties, but now, I was simply admitting that I alone was incapable of handling my prior life, one filled with frightening complications, some of which had taken root in my frailties, and others which had come about outside of myself. Submission became the conduit that brought me to Him, and still today, it saves me from falling into self-pity. My shattered feelings are slowly disappearing. It was necessary for me to experience the pain so that I could transcend it. Today, when talking of the pain, I have, with the sound advice of my friend, Joanne, replaced the word "my" with "the," because as she pointed it out to me, it is not "my" pain, it doesn't belong to me. The anger toward the pain has mellowed. It subsided only because God gave me the grace to deal with it. Amidst my confusion, my crumbling world and my so-called life, He replaced the bitterness and the cynicism in my heart with love, and I am eager to give it to all whom God places on my path.

I am now evolving into higher levels of unconditional love. I have overcome my cup! I am triumphant! I am breathing easier now, and I know with God's direction, I can try to help others emerge from their suffocating situation. I know that my odyssey with pain was not in vain. I was able to ascribe meaning, purpose, and dignity to it. Before now, I was unable to view it with hindsight. Now I see that my obstacles became my enlightenment. My hindrance became, in Tolkien's phrase, a "eucatastrophe," an event of unimaginable goodness. The pain propelled me into a process of transformation: my spiritual lethargy transpired into spiritual vigor; it became the instrument in fulfilling God's plan for me. Now I can say with ease that I am grateful for the pain, for only through my struggle with it was I able to find my identity with God. It allowed me to embark on a voyage of self-discovery. The affliction has helped me to hone my connectedness with Jesus. It unlocked the door to many answers I would not have otherwise received. Kristin Zambucka, in her book, *Ano Ano the Seed*, writes, "Your eyes will not really see until they are incapable of tears. Only when you can cry no more will you begin to grow." The affliction became meaningful only when I found myself enthralled in its coping stage and on my way to survival.

Ponder on this for a moment:

> There is no oil without squeezing the olives,
> No wine without pressing the grapes,
> No fragrance without crushing the flowers,
> And no real joy without sorrow.

Only because of the suffering am I now able to share my insights on pain, both physical and emotional, on the loss of self-esteem and self-regard, and on the feeling of death while still living.

Even when everything looks bad, God is good, and is all the time. Our situations are oftentimes engineered and used by the Lord to purify our life. The burdens, turmoil and trials somehow strengthen our relationships toward a new path. The friends who have abandoned and betrayed me, others who weren't there to support me, the colleagues who gossiped about me, the family members who disappointed me, my sons for whom I worried—all of these individuals helped me to let go of my selfish needs and to move forward on my own. My relationship with John, as dysfunctional as it was at times, allowed me to grow toward the Light. I am now becoming much closer to my family members, more now than I ever have been, and I feel they also are to me. The feeling of insecurity is disappearing, and one of trust and faith is rapidly growing. More than ever, I am experiencing His unconditional love.

I know that there are many fellow sufferers out there who can benefit from what I have lived and what I have learned. Most of all, I want to help them know, to see, and to believe that God will also help them to come out of the deep water in which they are drowning. He is the rock on which they can stand. He is the Only One Who can hold them up when they are torn apart by whatever problem. I learned that God's love does not keep us from trials, turmoil or tribulations, but that He does see us through them. Quoting from Billy Graham's, *Unto the Hill*, "God will not permit any troubles to come upon us, unless He has a specific plan by which great blessings can come out of the difficulty."

My storms have given me the potential to grow strong in my Christian walk. They have driven me deeper in Christ. God always makes a way when there seems to be none in sight. He holds us close by, and He guides us. He is the Only One, through His Holy Spirit, Who can give us the strength to surpass and to win battles. He can give to victims of circumstances the same inexhaustible treasures He gave me: the gift of beatitude, of inner peace where there are no limits, of inner fire and of inner healing where a circumcision of the heart occurs, whereby resulting in wholesome functioning. This inner healing disencumbers the guilt of the past, the concern of the present life, and the fear of the future.

Chapter X: Taking Hold

I am now back in the flow of life. The old cliché, "Go with the flow" (where I had been caught in its undertow), has become, "Flow with a glow!" and with the grace of God, I will be able to maintain the glow. My broken life is rapidly being recreated and remoulded by His hands. He is the Potter; I am the clay. He is the Only One Who will remold me into something simple, yet beautiful and precious in His eyes. It will be in the image of what He wants me to be. He is the Painter, Who, with His brush, will apply His colors onto me, one stroke at a time. He is the Artist; I am His canvas. I will become His work of art. His chisel will destroy the stone it cuts, and from it, He will fashion His likeness in and onto me. He is the Mason; I am His stone. He is the Sculptor; I am His piece of marble. God is working! God is moving! I will become His masterpiece

My ship has now reached shore, and as I disembark from it, I want to come aboard His vessel to be launched to the other side. I don't want to miss out on this exciting mystical journey. I want to partake in fellowship with Him. My own spirituality and my personal relationship with Jesus have become my essence. I have to remain in touch with this kinship because it means staying in touch with myself. He is the Author and the Finisher, the Alpha and the Omega! This is the start of the rest of my life!

I have learned while living in my own private pandemonium, with my wounds as companions, that I must stop looking back. Hurt makes us look into the past, but when you live through shame, grief, and trauma, you have to dedicate every effort toward victory. Your goal has to be to find a way to cross every bridge that closes down, to jump over every obstacle placed on your course, but you cannot attain this goal alone. God is the only requirement. The process of rebirth must occur. One must be born again; thus the labor begins! *A Course in Miracles* explains:

"To be born again is to let the past go, and to look without condemnation upon the present…You are but asked to let the future go, and place it in God's hands. And you will see by your experience, that you have laid the past and the present in His hands as well because the past will punish you no more, and the future dread will now be meaningless."

I will never resign again. I don't want to. There is too much to lose. I want to reach others and to share God's love with them. I want to show and prove to all who are hurting that I made it. The alchemy of my faith has turned me into a revivified victim.

I know that my own struggle to overcome this one season of my life makes me shine with a striking radiance and makes me set a higher value on every moment of my life. My appreciation of the better days and of the real moments that God is still giving me is much stronger now. Paul Brandt, author of *Pain: the Gift Nobody Wants*, sums it up perfectly. He writes, "The lack of pain makes it harder to enjoy pleasure."

Many people have noticed the change in me and say, "You look good, Diane. You seem to be more in control. There's a certain peace about you. You have some sort of glow. There's life in your eyes again. (Are not the eyes the windows of the soul?) You appear to be stronger. Your pain must be gone?" These comments are a bit puzzling to accept when you're not feeling your best physically. I'm often tempted to reply, "Do you want to know how I really feel?" I can say that my smile is no longer an artificial one; it is genuine; the love in my heart is unconditional, and the excitement I feel is not ephemeral, it is everlasting because I'm serving God, and He is real and permanent!

Until we know Jesus, God is but a mere abstraction. I do know that if the people who know me have Jesus in their life, if they have a personal relationship with Him, they know exactly how I feel; they don't need to ask me. But if they don't have Him, they cannot begin to imagine what it feels like to experience and to cherish the serenity, the joy, and the quality of life that can only come from Him. I can extol and unabashedly embrace the name of Jesus for all He's done for me. It is by His grace and by His mercy that I am saved! He is the Only One Who truly knows and understands what and how I feel!

In this world, we can work on becoming a spotless mirror in which the holiness of our Creator shines forth from us to all around us. We need to leave our mirror clean and clear of all the images of hidden darkness that we could have drawn upon it. It is only through His Word that we know what we really look like, and it is His statutes that show us how to spiritually groom ourselves.

Chapter XI: The Fruit Is in the Seed

"In order for a tree or any plant to grow and bear fruit, its seed must first be planted in the ground and die. In order for fruit to appear in our lives, we must first be planted in the Word of God and then die to self. In the face of chastening, adversity, discipline, and affliction, fruit begins to appear" (B. Graham, *Unto the Hills*).

God was removing the rocks. He was pulling out the weeds. He was breaking the ground. He was picking up the debris. He was sending his showers of virtues and blessings. I was now one of God's seedlings, and He was nurturing me in establishing a root system in His statutes. He was supplying the light of His truth as my source of energy. I was slowly starting to germinate, to branch out, and I would bear fruit. I was now entering a process of displacement. I was pulling off the "old" and putting on the "new." The hope of someday returning to my "old self" has now vanished. I will never go back to my "old self." The former Diane was sapped by illness, but the new me has experienced an exciting genesis via pain and spirituality. I walk with a new and different cadence and countenance. "I am a new creation; the old has gone, the new has come" (2 Corinthians 5:17). Thomas à Kempis' *Imitation of Christ* puts this in laymen's terms: "As iron put into fire is cleansed from rust and made all clear and pure, so truly a man who turns himself to God is purged from sloth and is suddenly changed into a new man."

I am fueled by a new Love, a new Identity, and with a new reliance on the One Whom I serve. I no longer have the need to understand or to make sense of the pain. I do not demand an explanation or a conclusion. I do not deny its presence, but I have come to terms with it. The "It" in my body somehow carries a golden key that I can use to open the door to a world of consciousness. I have learned to respect the pain. Now my need is to depend on Him, and He alone leads me out of bondage on to freedom.

The valuable messages emitted by the illness with its accompanying setbacks gave rise to thorough self-examination and taught me how to rid myself of the many toxins deteriorating my body, my mind, and my soul. It forced me to pay closer attention to the way my life was going, to the relationships I was in, and to myself—what I was all about.

It's true that I've made bad choices, made mistakes. Who hasn't? It's true that I've had bad times. Who hasn't? It's true that I've been hurt and deeply disappointed. Who hasn't? But Jesus has touched me, and He has loosed me from all that. Have you been touched and loosed by Him? I glorify Him, and I will never go back to the places where I've been! You can do the same if you have Jesus in your heart, in your life!

The horror movie of my experience has now been turned into a love story. I no longer feel threatened by the suffering. In the midst of my trial, our good Lord, Whose mercy endures forever, was doing something deeper in me: building a stronger character, stretching my capacity to believe Him and establishing stability in my life. God is the Salubrious Ingredient in my life. The Good Book has become the antidote that staves off my fear of pain, and my only medicine is love. My quality of life has been dramatically changed, whereas after the motorcycle accident, I first thought it had been reduced, only to realize that its quality has been greatly enhanced by another type of collision, one with my Saviour. There are no accidents with Him, only divine appointments. I am now experiencing a different "encounter": one of enormous love and reverence for everything around me. Pain has given coherence to my life. The tapestry of my prior life reveals a series of events that led to a higher place. I had to pursue an art I knew nothing about—one of accommodation. It was difficult to deal with the shame and the embarrassment of being less proficient in my performance and in my appearance. But I had to gracefully accept my limitations. I could no longer present myself as the conservatively well-dressed, ambitious, confident, and professional person that I once was. However, there are still those moments when I find myself rebelling against the accommodation by over-extending myself, only to pay dearly for my perfectionism. I had to cultivate clemency for certain traits of myself that I found loathsome: boring, unproductive, lacking energy, and unsociable. These unwelcomed characteristics of distress have allowed me to direct my focus away from my personal misery and to channel it to the needs of others. I had to learn to love myself first and, as a result, manifest love and kindness to my fellow man. In doing so, it is now easier for me to open my heart to God. If I did not believe in Yancey's statement, "There is no more effective healer than a wounded healer, and in the process, the wounded healer's scars may fade away," I would not have been able to rise above my world, which was heading toward complete havoc, and to write about it. I can only hope that the written experience of my disappointments and suffering will bring a ray of sunshine into the life of one who is hurting and is on the brink of despair. No one has to feel hopeless when hope is in God. It took me eight long years to learn what God wanted to teach me. Life is not a string of accidental circumstances; every event has a purpose.

The accident and its sequels have given me the opportunity to taste and to respond to the conflicting emotions of bitterness and compassion, of fragility and strength, of anger and love, of resentment and forgiveness, of indolence and perseverance, of pride and humility, of vanity and modesty, and of despondency and faith.

It took me these past eight years of my life to come to the conclusion that we cannot make successful plans alone. We need the Lord's guidance. T. Moore, in his book *Soul Mates*, states, "Struggling with the mysterious ways of fate may be the only path towards discovering that life is not a creation of our own will, but rather the crafting of a much greater will." I had to humble myself. I had dug my own well—did my own thing, my own way, in my own timing, and the end results had been disastrous; there was no water; the well was dry! I needed to acknowledge God in my life. I had to and wanted to care about what He thought, one way or the other.

The veil is lifted. The veneer is dropped. This new beginning is now the focal point of my curriculum. I now have a working relationship with Him. I often ask God what my purpose here is, and how I can best serve Him. Everything I do now, trivial as it may be, is synchronized with His plan. He is my Mentor. "I will instruct you and teach you in the way you should go; I will counsel you and watch over you" (Psalm 32:8).

I make it a point of asking myself in as many situations as I can, "What would Jesus do? How would He react, or would He? What would He say, and how would He say it? Or would He say nothing?" I wait for a check in my spirit that Only God gives me. I only want to move according to His plan, His timing. I try not to make any important decision without checking with my Heavenly Father, and He does check me and guides me with His Spirit whenever he sees me heading toward an inappropriate roadway. What kind of father would allow his son or daughter to go astray or to have harm come to him or her? God never leads us where His grace will not keep us.

My affliction became the impetus to the "new me." Quoting from Moore's *Soul Mates*, my new identity reflects "the Artemis elements in life, such as meditation, solitude, moral conviction, spiritual practice, and purity of life." This "new me" demonstrates a new compassion. Jesus says, "As he thinks in his heart, so is he" (Proverbs 23:7).

I like to think of myself as a peaceful observer. My attachment to things has been reduced. My need to feel needed is decreasing. I no longer have to prove myself. My emotional energy is no longer charged with judgment of others. I have become more indulgent of others. I try to respect those who are functioning at a different rhythm. My attitude toward my circumstances will determine my altitude. My capacity for a life of temperance, strength, and power has now taken a quantum leap. My self-defeating habits are replaced with self-enhancing ones; my ersatz behavior is being shaped into a more natural and calm state; my confusion is becoming clarity; my inner tumult is changing into an inner peace; my moments of darkness are being enlightened; my sorrow is overcome with genuine joy; my worries are slowly erased by faith and trust; my fears have abated; my anger is no longer. Love is dominant!

Chapter XII: Reaping with Joy

Today, I can accept the way I am. I never once envisaged a day where I would be forced to yield to mediocrity. Every single moment has to be good enough. I have to use the "now" the best way I know and learn to enjoy it. I have developed a way to adjust my intuitive antenna according to His signals. I'm turning the dial and tuning into God's channels. He's the One Who keeps my picture in focus. I exercise my positive thinking and use it as a guide which coaches my body. Our Good Lord gave me this body; therefore, I intend to treat it with respect, kindness, and love. I have no right to abuse it or to let it be ill-treated beyond its capacities.

My many stubborn and unsuccessful trials, and the many experiments of excess and relapse, have taught me that I am now able to curtail my activities and to follow my own path of moderation. Through these cycles, I have found a tolerable yet victorious way of living with the pain. I now have the ability to withdraw, to pause or to proceed, to ignore, reflect, or to check in with myself, to resist or to surrender. I have learned to own power. I have to honor my needs even if others disagree. I am no longer the chameleon I was, adapting my colors to my surroundings. I don't worry about others judging me, and my self-worth is no longer appraised by their value system. If I did, it would indicate that I doubt the value of God. I can now give myself the permission to say no to the people or to the things that interfere with the good functioning of my body, my mind, and my soul; it strengthens my integrity. I also have the authority to say yes to all those precious individuals and situations that nurture my body, my mind, and my soul.

Today, my present affection and my new addiction are with God, and my relationship with John is on hold. We have once more separated after recognizing and accepting the reality that we are on different paths. The love for each other remains, for we have learned to respect each other's dreams and aspirations. The one dream we always had was to move away to start a small business together just enough to sustain our everyday needs, but at this time, it does not seem feasible. I would like to do things right with the Lord; that is to marry, but John is not ready to make that commitment. And will he ever be? If God wills it, John and I will find each other again, and we will be on the same path because our relationship will have been blessed by God. If not, then so shall it be. Today, we remain the best of friends. The book *Illuminata* has left me this perfect prayer for John. I recite parts of it as often as I can.

> Dear God,
> "... May he fly free.
> May I appreciate the rightness of his need to travel.
> May I learn to respect his choices to go where he needs to go.
> If he finds another love, may that love flourish, for Your sake.
> Wherever he goes, dear Lord, please go with him.
> May he be blessed in all his doings.
> Please protect him.
> Bring him joy.
> May he always be happy.
> May he always be loved.
> May he find his way."

To this prayer I add this line of my own, "Lord, may he also find Your Way. Amen."

At times, when the pain does subside, I have much difficulty believing it is really happening; thus, I become suspicious of my body. Is it sending me mixed signals? However, on my "good" days, I escape for a short while into a world of numbness, and I savour its ecstasy. At times, I even want to believe that I am finally over the lingering fatigue and the discomfort, but reality quickly reappears as these temporary respites fade away and pain regains its entry. The feeling of euphoria reverts to a state of dysphoria.

For eight years I had frowned on God because I saw myself as an injured being. I read in one of my devotionals that God chooses what we go through and it's up to us to choose how we go through it. Since the beginning of time, God has given man the privilege of deciding to obey or to disobey. He does not want us to be robots, incapable of making choices. His love for us is so great that He doesn't restrict us by imposing His ways on us. He does, however, give us the freedom to choose, whether it be to accept Him or to say no to Him. With this freedom that He offers us to choose, we will undoubtedly make many mistakes. But I have learned through this long and agonizing trial that He forgives me and His love remains with me. My world of pain has driven me to God. He has used it as a megaphone to arouse me from my deep sleep, to awaken me, and to open my eyes to see the true meaning of life.

The injuries and the illness have made me more appreciative and reverent of the smaller things that do make a difference; I don't take things for granted anymore; rather, I count every blessing. I have the ability to see, to hear, to speak, to think, and to imagine; both of my arms function, and I have my two legs to walk on, even if I limp with my right one from time to time. The accident could have left me vegetable-like or living like a quadriplegic. All these gifts are from God. Too often, we do take them for granted. We must remember to keep thanking and praising Him for the many lessons and graces He gives us, and for the ones that are to come. I am learning to be content with less and to delight in simpler things. I had never had, nor taken the time to take a good look at or to lend an ear to God's work in nature. I have started enjoying the magic of flowers, the changing color of leaves, the sweet melody of birds serenading in the early morning hours, the soothing sound of raindrops tapping on the window pane, the crispness of snow, the texture of grass, the splendor of sunrises and the magnificence of sunsets, even the howling of the wind, the sound of young children laughing, and the friendly smile of a stranger.

Today, I try to mediate and to pray each morning. When I pray, I talk to God. When I meditate, I listen to what He has to say. I need and crave the silence. It helps me to reconnect with my source of energy, which, in turn, guides me to redesign my life. The reading of the Word is an important part of my daily agenda; it serves as a panacea. I always manage to fall on a scripture or thought that is comforting, and that gives me hope and power for the day. What we put in our mind is what will come out.

I also exercise three times weekly, and I make an effort of going for a walk every day. I find walking alone helps me to get in touch with my sacred self. I like to walk using in cadence with my steps, a variety of mantra-like words or phrases such as: "Love/Truth/Joy/Peace" or "Thy/Will/Be/Done" or "Thank/You/Jesus" or "God/You're/In/Control," and often I say, "Guard/My/Heart/Guard/My/Mind." They become body rhythm prayers. During inclement weather, I force myself to walk around every room in my apartment or try to use the stairs in the building.

My need to mask the pain is no longer because my inner strength and my quietude of inward acquiescence are indicative of my control over it. Today,

I still have the pain, but it no longer owns me. I am convinced that by shifting my consciousness to a spiritual mode; I can and will, in time, and with God's grace, achieve a state of well-being.

I agree with Barasch in his book, *The Healing Path*, when he says, "The deeper issue is not whether someone will be cured, but whether they're going to resolve their life, whether they're going to change. To me, that's what healing's all about." I have learned that it is not so much our circumstances that dictate their results on us, positive or negative, but rather how we relate to them and how we handle them.

How do I really feel today? I still have my days when everything looks bleak. At times, I am like Humpty Dumpty, that no one or nothing can put back together the broken pieces, except the King Himself. Other times, I feel like a kite made of a soft, thin, pliable membrane, and not from the usual paper. Both of these textures rip, but the membrane is like skin that lives and breathes. I am like that membrane kite floating around in limbo. Sometimes I fly high; other times I fly low. When the breeze is soft and gentle, I glide freely, but when the barometric pressures of my daily living are characterized by irregular up and down currents, my flight is disrupted. If the conditions bring about a stronger force, my struggle to stay in flight becomes even more challenging, and at times, I fall to the ground, only to be picked up each time by His gentle hand, to be propelled once more and to continue soaring. I learned to abandon my inadequate self-sufficiency and to rely on God's unlimited power. When I keep my eyes focused on the Lord rather than on my circumstances, I know from Isaiah 40:31 that, "Those who hope in the Lord will renew their strength, They will soar on wings like eagles; they will run and not grow weary, they will walk and not be faint." He also gave me a map—the Bible—His love letters. His Word comes with complete instructions, directions, and a compass on how to reach my destination. His Word is specific. It gives me a clear-cut path, a highway to follow, and there is no confusion. I may still be tempted to go on neighboring tangent roads, but I know that my Road Master will always being me back to the Main Highway if I abide by His safety rules.

I know I am still vulnerable and feeble; that is why my prayers never cease. They are sometimes aggressive prayers, only because I not only strive and struggle to find His Will for my life, but I place the burden on Him. My petitions can only make me ascend to higher levels of awareness. I know He answers my prayers, but I have had to learn painfully that both faith and patience are needed in my requests. I have to trust Him, for He has His own timing. I have decided to be in harmony with myself and with my surroundings. I feel fully equipped to brave the elements of my physical world because I know I have His infinite invisible force within me. The sap is flowing! My hope and my strength are in Christ my Lord. I feel assured that the Good Lord asks nothing of me, for the time being, but simply to praise and worship Him. I am following the arrow on my new path that says, "You are here," and His Word that says, "Your ears shall hear a word behind you, saying, 'This is the way, walk in it'" (Isaiah 30:21). I believe He accepts me where I'm at today, foibles and all. I have entered a new frontier.

> "I am not what I ought to be;
> I am not what I would like to be;
> I am not what I hope to be,
> But I am not what I once was,
> and by the grace of God, I am what I am."
> —John Newton (1725-1807)

The battles are still on, and mediocrity in worldly routines is something I've had to accept, but my walk with God aims at a quality of excellence! A victim, I am no longer; a victor, I shall remain!

> "Victory comes through defeat;
> healing through brokenness;
> finding self through losing self."
> —C. Colson

By accepting the love of Jesus Christ in my life, I will be able to do all that He asks of me. We are on each other's side.

I'm repeating the adage used earlier in my story, "Home is where the heart is," but this time it is applied in a different context. My heart is with my Creator, Who is my Father, my Protector, my Liberator, my Redeemer, my Saviour, my Fortress. He is my Haven, and I am the prodigal daughter. I have come home; I am home!

> Dear God,
> I was lost; You brought me Home. Thank you.
> I was in darkness; You revealed the Light. Thank you.
> I was trapped in a maze; You showed me the Way. Thank you.

I lived in obscurity; You gave me Lucidity. Thank you.
I was addicted; You provided Deliverance. Thank you.
I was a teacher; You made me a Student. Thank You.
I was ambitious; You bestowed me with simplicity. Thank you.
I was confused; You gave me Truth. Thank you.
I was bitter; You poured out your Compassion. Thank you.
I felt resentment; You taught me Forgiveness. Thank you.
I was weak; You gave me Strength. Thank you.
I was unstable; You made me Secure. Thank you.
I was sick; You gave me my Healing. Thank you.
I walked in pride; You taught me Humility. Thank you.
I was cold and dull; You stirred me to Fervor of spirit. Thank you.
I was in doubt; You refined my Faith. Thank you.
I lived in guilt; You demonstrated your Grace. Thank you.
I felt tumult; You made me feel Peace. Thank you.
I felt sorrow; You made me feel Joy. Thank you.
I was despondent; You gave me Hope. Thank you.
I was angry, and you taught me unconditional Love. Thank you.
And now, dear Lord, let me be and do for You. Amen.

You will only know and understand how and what I feel when you receive and accept the same gift I have, and that gift is Jesus. I give Him all the praise, the honor, and the glory that only He is worthy of receiving!

Epilogue

This gift that I was given to triumph over the losses in my life can be received by anyone who is ready to humbly admit that overcoming and accepting challenges cannot be done alone. Desperation will most times lead us to reach out to something bigger than oneself. God's message to us is not "Do this and don't do that," but simply, "Come to Me."

I leave you with a simple prayer, and I assure you that if it said sincerely from your heart that, not only will your circumstance change, but so will you.

Jesus, I come to you now and recognize that You have paid my debt at the cross. I confess all my past sins and ask for your forgiveness. I invite you to come into my heart and to change me. Make me a new person. I thank you for wiping the slate clean and for giving me a brand new start. Help me through the process of overcoming my own challenges. Amen.

Bibliography

Barasch, Marc, *The Healing Path: A Soul Approach to Illness*, Ned Leavitt Agency, Copyright © 1993. Used by permission.

Brand, Dr. Paul and Yancey, Philip, *Pain: The Gift Nobody Wants*, Harper Collins Publishers Inc., Copyright © 1993. Used by permission.

Brand, Dr. Paul and Yancey, Philip, *In His Image*, Copyright © 1984, Zondervan Publishing. Used by permission of The Zondervan Corporation.

Chambers, Oswald, *My Utmost for His Highest*, Copyright © 1935 by Dodd Mead & Co., renewed © 1963 by the Oswald Publications Assn., Ltd., and is used by permission of Discovery House Publishers, Box 3566, Grand Rapids, MI 49501. All rights reserved.

Colson, Charles, *Loving God*, Copyright © 1983, 1987, Zondervan Publishing. Used by permission of The Zondervan Corporation.

Cliffe, Albert E., *Let Go and Let God*, Prentice Hall Press, New York, 1993.

Graham, Billy, *Unto the Hills*, Copyright © 1996, Thomas Nelson Publishing Group, Vancouver, BC. Used by permission.

Jung, Carl, *The Collected Works of C.J. Jung*, vol.13, Copyright ©1968, Princeton University Press. Used by permission.

Kempis, Thomas à, *Imitation of Christ*, Copyright © 1955, Random House. Used by permission.

Lorde, Audre, *A Burst of Light*, Copyright © 1988, Firebrand Books Crossing Press.

Merriam-Webster, A., *Webster's New Collegiate Dictionary*, G.&G Merriam Company, Springfield, MA 1981.

Molière, *The Imaginary Invalid*, Copyright © 1950, 1957, 1959, 1960, Samuel French Ltd., London, UK. Used by permission.

Moore, Thomas, *Soul Mates: Honoring the Mysteries of Love and Relationships*. Copyright © 1994, Harper Collins Publishers, Inc. Used by permission.

Newton, John, *Out of the Depths*, attributed to John Newton.

Norwood, Robin, *Why Me, Why This, Why Now*, McClleland & Stewart, Ltd., Copyright © 1994, Toronto, ON. Used by permission.

Schuller, Robert H., *Life's Not Fair but God Is Good*, Copyright © 1993, Crystal Cathedral Ministries, Garden Grove, CA.

Foundation for A Course in Miracles, Copyright © 1975, Temecula CA. Used by permission.

The New Student Bible, Zondervan Publishing House, 1986.

Williamson, Marianne, *Illuminata: Thoughts, Prayers, Rites of Passage*, Copyright © 1994, Random House, New York. Used by permission of Random House, Inc..

Yancey, Philip, *Where Is God When it Hurts*, Copyright © 1977, 1990. Zondervan Publishing. Used by permission of The Zondervan Corporation.

Zambucka, Kristin, *Ano Ano the Seed*, Copyright © 1978, Booklines Hawaii Ltd. Used by permission.

Printed in the United States
45219LVS00004B/107